I love you, I have loved

사랑한다, 나는 사랑을 가졌다

I Love you, I have Loved

사랑한다,
나는 사랑을 가졌다

나태주 Na Tae-ju | 안선재 Brother Anthony of Taizé

내가 꾸는 마지막 꿈

내가 어려서 가진 꿈 가운데 가장 이루기 어려운 꿈은 시인이 되는 꿈이며 그 꿈은 여전히 현재 진행형이라고 보아집니다. 거기에 더하여, 나는 한글로 쓰여진 나의 시를 세계 각국의 젊은 독자들이 읽어주기를 바라는 새로운 꿈을 갖게 되었습니다.

이미 여러 나라에 나의 시집이 번역된 바 있으나, 영어로 번역된 시집이 한 권도 없어 아쉽고 그립던 차에 권위 있는 영문 번역가이신 앤서니 수사님을 소개받아 영어 번역 시집이 이렇게 나오게 되었습니다. 여간 기쁘고 감사한 일이 아닙니다.

번역은 또 하나의 창작이라고 합니다. 한국의 시인이 한글로 쓴 시를 그 시인의 어투와 말맛까지 살려서 번역하기는 매우 어려웠을 것으로 압니다. 번역하신 앤서니 수사님께 새삼스럽게 감사를 드리며 이 번역 시집이 영어를 사용하는 세계인들의 손에 들어가 그들로부터 사랑받는 시집이 되기를 소망합니다. 그것이 내가 꾸는 마지막 꿈입니다.

2025년 신춘
나태주 씁니다.

My Last Dream

Among the dreams I had as a child, the most difficult to achieve was the dream of becoming a poet, and that dream is still ongoing. In addition, now I have a new dream of having young readers from all over the world read my poetry written in Korean.

My poetry collections have already been translated in many countries. However, I was sad as I longed for a single poetry collection translated into English, and at last I was introduced to Brother Anthony, an experienced English translator, and now this English-translated poetry collection has been published. I am so happy and grateful. They say translation is another form of creation. I know it must be very difficult to translate poems written in Korean while preserving the poet's tone and voice. I would like to express my gratitude to Brother Anthony for translating my poems, and I hope that this collection will be loved by English-speaking people around the world. That is my last dream.

New Year 2025
Written by Na Tae-ju

Seeking life's beauty and meaning

Na Tae-ju lives in Gongju, a small, historic town in the center of South Korea. He was a school teacher and headmaster there, and is acclaimed there as the town's major living celebrity. His poems are loved in Korea by many for whom other poets' work is too complex or challenging. He speaks directly in the simplest ways to peoples' deepest yearnings for beauty and meaning. This is made possible by his own hidden knowledge of pain and darkness. I was belatedly introduced to his work by friends who begged me to translate into English his most widely loved poems. This collection is the result and I hope that through these translated poems many will discover the poet's vision and sensitive evocation of life's beauty and meaning.

Brother Anthony of Taizé

삶의 아름다움과 의미를 찾아

나태주 시인은 한국 중부의 작고 아늑하며 역사적인 도시 공주에 살고 있습니다. 시인은 그곳에서 학교 교사와 교장을 지냈으며, 공주에 거주하는 시인 셀럽으로 유명합니다. 시는 복잡하고 어려운 것이라고 생각해온 많은 한국인들이 그의 시를 사랑합니다. 시인은 삶의 아름다움과 의미를 꾸밈없는 단순한 시어들로 이야기합니다. 시인이 인간의 고통과 어둠에 대한 깊은 인식과 통찰력을 가지고 있기 때문입니다. 나는 사실 오랫동안 모르고 지냈던 나태주 시인의 시들을 친한 지인들을 통해서 알게 되었습니다. 많은 지인들이 한국인에게 가장 사랑받는 그의 시들을 영어로 번역해 달라고 계속 간청했기 때문입니다. 저의 뒤늦은 나태주 시인 읽기의 결과물이 이 시집입니다. 영어로 표현된 나태주 시인의 시들을 통해 많은 사람들이 삶의 아름다움과 의미를 이야기하는 시인의 통찰력과 섬세한 시어들을 느끼길 바랍니다.

안선재 수사

차례 | contents

마음속에 시 하나 싹텄습니다
A poem sprouted in my heart

어린 낙타 1 · Young Camel 1 __ 18

어린 낙타 2 · Young Camel 2 __ 22

시인 · A Poet __ 24

시인 2 · Poet 2 __ 26

돌멩이 · A Pebble __ 28

내가 좋아하는 사람 · The Person I Like __ 30

몸 · The Body __ 32

시 1 · Poem 1 __ 36

시 2 · Poem 2 __ 38

시 3 · Poem 3 __ 40

여행 2 · Journey 2 __ 42

서정시인 · The Lyric Poet __ 44

시인학교 · Poetry School __ 46

지상에서의 며칠 · A Few Days on Earth __ 48

동행 · Companionship __ 50

묘비명 · Epitaph __ 52

기도의 자리 · A Place for Prayer __ 54

사랑한다, 나는 사랑을 가졌다
I love you, I have loved

사랑은 언제나 서툴다 · Love Is Always Awkward __ 58

사랑 1 · Love 1 __ 60

사랑 3 · Love 3 __ 62

사랑 4 · Love 4 __ 64

우리들의 푸른 지구 2 · Our Blue Earth 2 __ 66

눈 위에 쓴다 · Writing on Snow __ 68

마음을 얻다 · Gaining a Heart __ 70

먼 길 · A Long Journey __ 72

너를 두고 · Leaving You __ 74

끝끝내 · Ultimately __ 76

네가 있어 · Since You Are __ 78

늦여름 · Late Summer __ 80

별것도 아닌 사랑 · Love, That's Nothing Special __ 82

행복 2 · Happiness 2 __ 86

유월에 · In June __ 88

연 · Lotus __ 90

초라한 고백 · A Humble Confession __ 92

의자 · A Chair __ 94

여행의 끝 · Journey's End __ 96

장식 · Decoration __ 98

그래도 · Still __ 100

좋다 · Good __ 102

말랑말랑 · Soft and Fluffy __ 104

호명 · Calling Your Name __ 106

한 사람 · One Person __ 108

모두 떠난 자리에 · The Place Everyone Has Left __ 110

당신 · You __ 112

사랑은 그런 것 · Love Is Like That __ 114

사랑에 답함 · Responding to Love __ 116

꽃 1 · Flower 1 __ 118

꽃 2 · Flower 2 __ 120

꽃 3 · Flower 3 __ 122

한밤중에 · In the Middle of the Night __ 124

오늘의 꽃 · Today's Flower __ 126

들길을 걸으며 · Walking Along a Field Path __ 128

산수유꽃 진 자리 · The Place where Cornelian Cherry Blossoms Fell __ 132

사랑이여 조그만 사랑이여 · Love, Little Love __ 134

잠시 머물다 가기에 사랑이다
Lingering for a while then leaving, that is love

안개 · Fog __ 138

작별 · Farewell __ 140

공항 · Airport __ 142

별리 · Separation __ 144

바람에게 묻는다 · Asking the Wind __ 146

나무 · A Tree __ 148

그런 사람으로 · Someone Like That __ 150

사람 그리워 · Longing for People __ 152

섬 · An Island __ 154

동백 · The Camellia __ 156

인생 3 · Life 3 __ 158

사막 · The Desert __ 160

그래 · Yes __ 162

꽃구경 · Viewing Flowers __ 164

제비꽃 · Violets __ 166

쓸쓸한 여름 · A Solitary Summer __ 168

붓꽃 · Iris __ 170

들국화 1 · Wild Chrysanthemum 1 __ 174

들국화 2 · Wild Chrysanthemum 2 __ 176

들국화 3 · Wild Chrysanthemum 3 __ 180

대숲 아래서 · Under the Bamboo Grove __ 182

재회 1 · Reunion 1 __ 186

아직도 · Still Now __ 188

이 가을에 · This Autumn __ 190

그리움 1 · Longing 1 __ 192

그리움 2 · Longing 2 __ 194

그리움 3 · Longing 3 __ 196

이별 · Parting __ 198

오늘도 그대는 멀리 있다
Today, too, You Are Far Away

바람 부는 날 · A Windy Day __ 202

부탁 · A Request __ 204

사는 법 · How to Live __ 206

떠나와서 · After Leaving __ 208

오지 못하는 마음 · A Heart That Can't Come __ 210

사랑하는 마음 내게 있어도 · Even Though I Have a Loving Heart __ 212

미루나무 · The Willow Tree __ 216

개양귀비 · Poppies __ 218

편지 · A Letter __ 220

부탁이야 · Please __ 222

그 말 · Those Words __ 226

오늘도 그대는 멀리 있다 · Today, too, You Are Far Away __ 228

마지막 기도 · Last Prayer __ 230

멀리서 빈다 · Praying from Afar __ 232

겨울에도 꽃 핀다 · Flowers Bloom Even in Winter __ 234

연꽃 · A Lotus __ 238

내가 너를 · I and You __ 240

안부 · Greetings __ 242

꽃이 되어 새가 되어
Becoming a Flower, Becoming a Bird

꽃이 되어 새가 되어 · Becoming a Flower, Becoming a Bird __ 246

풀꽃 1 · Wildflower 1 __ 248

풀꽃 2 · Wildflower 2 __ 250

풀꽃 3 · Wildflower 3 __ 252

혼자서 · Alone __ 254

앉은뱅이 꽃 · A Squat Flower __ 256

봄비 · Spring Rain __ 258

어린 벗에게 · To a Young Friend __ 260

너무 잘하려고 애쓰지 마라 · Don't Try too Hard __ 262

꽃필 날 · The Day Flowers Bloom __ 264

잘람잘람 · Brimming __ 266

아끼지 마세요 · Don't Be Stingy __ 268

좋은 날 하자 · Let's Have a Good Day __ 272

좋은 날 · A Good Day __ 274

게으름 연습 · Practicing Laziness __ 276

꽃밭에서 · In the Flowerbed __ 280

오늘의 약속 · Today's Promise __ 282

선물 1 · Gift 1 __ 286

오늘 · Today __ 288

행복 1 · Happiness 1 __ 290

그럼에도 불구하고 · Nonetheless __ 292

그가 섭섭하게 대해 줄 때 · When They Treat Me Badly __ 296

뒷모습 1 · Back view 1 __ 298

노래 방울 · Song Drops __ 300

산수유 · Cornelian Cherry __ 304

너는 별이다 · You Are a Star __ 306

해설 지친 마음 곁에 피어난 풀꽃 한 송이
  박재섭(인제대 명예교수, 국문학) __ 308

  A Wildflower Blooming Next to a Tired Heart
  Park Jae-seop(Emeritus Professor, Korean Literature,
  Inje University) __ 317

마음속에 시 하나 싹텄습니다

A poem sprouted in my heart

어린 낙타 1

마음속에 낙타 한 마리
살고 있었네
어리고도 순한 낙타
세상물정 모르고
오직 세상한테
사랑받기만을 꿈꾸던 낙타

쉽사리 세상한테
사랑받을 수 없었네
타박타박 걸으며 걸으며
어른 낙타가 되었고
늙은 낙타가 되었네

가도 가도 목마른 날들
팍팍한 발걸음
세상은 또 하나의 사막
어디에도 쉴 만한 그늘은 없고
주저앉을 의자 하나
마련되어 있지 않았네

Young Camel 1

A camel lived in my heart,
a young and gentle camel,
ignorant of the ways of the world,
a camel that only dreamed
of being loved by the world

It could not easily
be loved by the world.
Walking step by step,
it became an adult camel
then an old camel.

On thirsty days,
no matter how far it walked,
plodding on,
the world was just another desert,
no shade to rest in,
no chair to sit down on.
Today, too, an old camel walks across the desert

오늘도 늙은 낙타 사막을 가네

물 없는 길 사랑 없는 길
세상한테 사랑받고 싶은 마음 하나
세상 속으로 길 떠나네
사막의 길 걷고 또 걷네.

Paths without water,

paths without love,

with a heart that longs to be loved by the world,

setting out into the world,

it walks on and on along a desert road.

어린 낙타 2

날마다 네 마음속
어린 낙타 한 마리를 깨워
길을 떠나라
아직은 어린 낙타이니
그의 등에 올라타지는 말고
옆에 서서 함께 걸어라
낙타가 걸으면 걷고
낙타가 쉬면 쉬고
낙타가 바라보는 곳을
따라서 바라볼 일이다
때로는 낙타가 뜯어먹는
낙타 풀도 먹어야 하겠지만
부디 입술이나 잇몸에서
피가 나지 않도록 조심해라
네 마음속 어린 낙타 한 마리가
너의 스승이며 이웃이며
처음이자 마지막
길동무임을 잊지 말아라.

Young Camel 2

Every day, wake up the young camel

in your heart and set out on a journey.

It is still a young camel,

so do not climb on its back,

but just stand beside it and walk together.

Walk when the camel walks,

rest when the camel rests,

and look where the camel is looking.

Sometimes you have to eat the grass

that the camel eats, but be careful

not to let your lips or gums bleed.

Do not forget

that the young camel in your heart

is your teacher, your neighbor,

your first and last companion.

시인

마음이 아파서 여러 번
글씨 쓰는 손이 떨렸습니다.

A Poet

My heart ached so much

that my hand shook several times as I wrote.

시인 2

두리번거리다가
한발 늦고

망설이다가
한발 늦고

구름 보고 웃다가
꽃을 보며 좋아서

날 저물어서야
울먹인 아이

빈손으로 혼자서
돌아온 아이.

Poet 2

A child who looked around and was one step behind,
who hesitated and was one step behind,

who laughed at clouds and was happy with flowers,
who only cried when the sun set.

A child who returned home
alone and empty-handed.

돌멩이

흐르는 맑은 물결 속에 잠겨
보일 듯 말 듯 일렁이는
얼룩무늬 돌멩이 하나
돌아가는 길에 가져가야지
집어 올려 바위 위에
놓아두고 잠시
다른 볼일 보고 돌아와
찾으려니 도무지
어느 자리에 두었는지
찾을 수가 없다

혹시 그 돌멩이, 나 아니었을까?

A Pebble

One spotted pebble

seemed to ripple

in the clear flowing stream.

Deciding to take it back with me,

I picked it up and put it on a rock.

I went to do something else for a moment

and when I came back looking for it,

I couldn't find it.

Could that pebble have been me?

내가 좋아하는 사람

내가 좋아하는 사람은
슬퍼할 일을 마땅히 슬퍼하고
괴로워할 일을 마땅히 괴로워하는 사람.

남의 앞에 섰을 때
교만하지 않고
남의 뒤에 섰을 때
비굴하지 않은 사람.

내가 좋아하는 사람은
미워할 것을 마땅히 미워하고
사랑할 것을 마땅히 사랑하는
그저 보통의 사람.

The Person I Like

The person I like

is someone who is rightly sad about things that are sad,

who is rightly pained by things that are painful,

Someone not arrogant

when standing before others,

not servile

when standing behind others.

The person I like

is someone who rightly dislikes what should be disliked,

who rightly loves what should be loved,

simply an ordinary person.

몸

아침저녁 맑은 물로
깨끗하게 닦아주고
매만져 준다
당분간은 내가 신세지며
살아야 할 사글세방
밤이면 침대에 반듯이 눕혀
재워도 주고
낮이면 그럴 듯한 옷으로
치장해 주기도 하고
더러는 병원이나 술집에도
데리고 다닌다
처음에는 내 집인 줄 알았지
살다보니 그만 전셋집으로 바뀌더니
전세 돈이 자꾸만 오르는 거야
견디다 못해 전세 돈 빼어
이제는 사글세로 사는 신세가 되었지
모아둔 돈은 줄어들고
방세는 점점 오르고
그러나 어쩌겠나

The Body

I wash it clean with clear water

every morning and evening

and look after it.

For the time being, it will have to live

at my expense in a rented house.

At night, I will lay it flat on the bed

and let it sleep.

During the day, I will dress it up in nice clothes,

sometimes I will take it to the hospital or a bar.

At first, I thought it was my house,

but as I lived there, it turned into a key-money house,

and the cost kept going up.

I couldn't stand it anymore,

so I took back the key money

and now I live in a rented house.

The money I saved is decreasing

and the cost keeps going up,

but what can I do?

For the time being, it's the house I have to live in.

당분간은 내가 신세져야 할
나의 집
아침저녁 맑은 물로 깨끗하게
씻어주고 닦아준다.

I wash it clean with clear water

every morning and evening

and rub it.

시 1

마당을 쓸었습니다
지구 한 모퉁이가 깨끗해졌습니다

꽃 한 송이 피었습니다
지구 한 모퉁이가 아름다워졌습니다

마음 속에 시 하나 싹텄습니다
지구 한 모퉁이가 밝아졌습니다

나는 지금 그대를 사랑합니다
지구 한 모퉁이가 더욱 깨끗해지고
아름다워졌습니다.

Poem 1

I swept the yard.

A corner of the Earth became clean

A flower bloomed.

A corner of the Earth became beautiful

A poem sprouted in my heart.

A corner of the Earth became bright

I love you now.

A corner of the Earth has become cleaner

and more beautiful.

시 2

그냥 줍는 것이다

길거리나 사람들 사이에
버려진 채 빛나는
마음의 보석들.

Poem 2

I'm just picking up

The sparkling jewels
of the heart
abandoned in the streets or among the crowds.

시 3

만나기는 한나절이었지만
잊기에는 평생도 모자랐다.

Poem 3

We only met for half a day,

but a lifetime was not long enough to forget.

여행 2

떠나 온 곳으로 다시는
돌아갈 수 없다는 걸 알기까지는
많은 시간이 필요했다.

Journey 2

It took me a long time

to realize that I could never return

to the place I had left.

서정시인

다른 아이들 모두 서커스 구경 갈 때
혼자 남아 집을 보는 아이처럼
모로 돌아서서 까치집을 바라보는
늙은 화가처럼
신도들한테 따돌림당한
시골 목사처럼.

The Lyric Poet

Like a child who is left alone to guard the house

while all the other children go to the circus;

like an old painter who turns

and looks at a magpie's nest;

like a country pastor

ostracized by his followers.

시인학교

남의 외로움 사 줄 생각은 하지 않고
제 외로움만 사 달라 조른다
모두가 외로움의 보따리 장수.

Poetry School

They don't think about buying other people's
loneliness,
they only ask people to buy their loneliness.
Everyone is a peddler of loneliness.

지상에서의 며칠

때 절은 종이 창문 흐릿한 달빛 한줌이었다가
바람 부는 들판의 키 큰 미루나무 잔가지 흔드는 바람이었다가
차마 소낙비일 수 있었을까? 겨우
옷자락이나 머리칼 적시는 이슬비였다가
기약 없이 찾아든 바닷가 민박집 문지방까지 밀려와
칭얼대는 파도 소리였다가
누군들 안 그러랴
잠시 머물고 떠나는 지상에서의 며칠, 이런 저런 일들
좋았노라 슬펐노라 고달팠노라
그대 만나 잠시 가슴 부풀고 설렜었지
그리고는 오래고 긴 적막과 애달픔과 기다림이 거기 있었지
가는 여름 새끼손톱에 스며든 봉숭아 빠알간 물감이었다가
잘려 나간 손톱조각에 어른대는 첫눈이었다가
눈물이 고여서였을까? 눈썹
깜짝이다가 눈썹 두어 번 깜짝이다가…….

A Few Days on Earth

At times, it was a handful of hazy moonlight on a dusty paper window,
then the wind swaying the branches of a tall zelkova tree in a windy field,
or might it have been a shower? At least a drizzle
that barely wet the hem of my clothes or my hair,
then it was the sound of waves that came without warning
and whined at the threshold of a seaside guesthouse.
Wouldn't anyone be the same?
A few days on earth where I stayed for a while before leaving,
things that were good, sad, and hard.
When I met you, my heart swelled
and fluttered for a moment,
then there was a long, long silence, full of sorrow, and waiting.
The bright red juice of a balsam flower
soaking into my fingernails in the passing summer,
then the first snow falling on a scrap of my cut fingernail.
Was it because tears were gathering?
I blinked my eyes, blinked twice…

동행

어머니는 언제 죽나?
내가 죽을 때 죽지.

Companionship

When will Mother die?
She will die when I die.

묘비명

많이 보고 싶겠지만
조금만 참자.

Epitaph

You must long to see me again,
but let's wait a little longer.

기도의 자리

눈물 나리
하늘의 별 하나 밤을 새워
나를 보고 반짝인다
생각해봐

눈물 나리
어딘가 나 한 사람 위해
누군가 울고 있다
생각해봐

처음부터 기도는
거기에 있었다.

A Place for Prayer

When tears flow
only think
that a star in the sky stays up all night
looking down at me and shining.

When tears flow,
only think
that somewhere, someone is crying
for me alone.

From the very beginning, prayer
was there.

사랑한다, 나는 사랑을 가졌다

I love you, I have loved

사랑은 언제나 서툴다

서툴지 않은 사랑은 이미
사랑이 아니다
어제 보고 오늘 보아도
서툴고 새로운 너의 얼굴

낯설지 않은 사랑은 이미
사랑이 아니다
금방 듣고 또 들어도
낯설고 새로운 너의 목소리

어디서 이 사람을 보았던가…
이 목소리 들었던가…
서툰 것만이 사랑이다
낯선 것만이 사랑이다

오늘도 너는 내 앞에서
다시 한 번 태어나고
오늘도 나는 네 앞에서
다시 한 번 죽는다.

Love Is Always Awkward

Love that is not awkward

is no longer love.

Your face is always awkward and new,

even when I see it yesterday and today.

Love that is not unfamiliar

is no longer love.

Your voice that is always unfamiliar and new,

even when I hear it over and over again.

Have I seen this person somewhere…

Have I heard this voice somewhere…

Only awkwardness is love.

Only unfamiliarity is love.

Today, you are born again

in front of me,

and today I die again

in front of you.

사랑 1

빛과 함께 온다
소리와 함께 온다
향기와 함께 온다
웃음과 함께 온다
그런 것은
눈물을 남기며 사라진다
바다가 되지도 못하면서
가슴속에 몇 알갱이
소금을 남긴다.

Love 1

It comes with light.

It comes with sound.

It comes with fragrance.

It comes with laughter.

Then it

vanishes, leaving tears behind.

Without becoming the sea

it leaves behind

a few grains of salt in the heart.

사랑 3

사랑할까봐 겁나요, 당신
언젠가 당신 미워할지도 모르고
헤어질지도 몰라서지요

미워할까 겁나요, 당신
미워하는 마음 옹이가 되어 내가
나를 더 미워할 것만 같아서지요

이제는 당신 사랑하지 않는 것이
나의 사랑이어요.

Love 3

I'm afraid of loving you,
because I might hate you someday
and we might break up.

I'm afraid of hating you,
because I think my hatred for you
will make me hate myself even more.

Now, not loving you
is my love.

사랑 4

우연히 내 안에
들어온 너, 처음엔
탁구공만 하더니

점점 자라서
나보다 더 커지고
지구만큼 자라버렸네

너를 안아본다
지구를 안아본다.

Love 4

You came into me

by chance, at first

you were just a ping-pong ball,

But you grew bigger,

bigger than me,

grew as big as the Earth.

As I hug you

I hug the Earth.

우리들의 푸른 지구 2

사랑한다는 말 대신에 하는 말
우리 오래 만나자

사랑하겠다는 말 대신에 하는 대답
우리 함께 오래 있어요

날마다 푸른 지구
내일 더욱 푸른 지구

오늘은 네가 나에게 지구이고
내가 너에게 지구이다.

Our Blue Earth 2

What we say instead of saying 'I love you':
Let's meet for a long time.

Our answer instead of saying 'I love you':
Let's stay together for a long time.

Every day the Earth is blue,
tomorrow the Earth will be bluer.

Today, you are the Earth to me
and I am the Earth to you.

눈 위에 쓴다

눈 위에 쓴다
사랑한다 너를
그래서 나 쉽게
지구라는 아름다운 별
떠나지 못한다.

Writing on Snow

I write on snow:

I love you,

so I can't easily leave

this beautiful planet

called Earth.

마음을 얻다

있는 것도 없다고
네가 말하면
없는 것이고

없는 것도 있다고
네가 말하면
있는 것이다

후회하지 않겠다.

Gaining a Heart

If you say that even what's there is not there,
then it's not there.

If you say that what's not there is there,
then it's there.

I won't regret it.

먼 길

함께 가자
먼 길

너와 함께라면
멀어도 가깝고

아름답지 않아도
아름다운 길

나도 그 길 위에서
나무가 되고

너를 위해 착한
바람이 되고 싶다.

A Long Journey

Let's go together,
on a long journey.

If I'm with you,
even far is near.

Even if it's not beautiful,
it will be a beautiful journey.

I want to become
a tree on that road,

Want to become
a good wind for you.

너를 두고

세상에 와서
내가 하는 말 가운데서
가장 고운 말을
너에게 들려주고 싶다

세상에 와서
내가 가진 생각 가운데서
가장 예쁜 생각을
너에게 주고 싶다

세상에 와서
내가 할 수 있는 표정 가운데
가장 좋은 표정을
너에게 보이고 싶다

이것이 내가 너를
사랑하는 진정한 이유
나 스스로 네 앞에서 가장
좋은 사람이 되고 싶은 소망이다.

Leaving You

I want to tell you

the most beautiful words

I have ever spoken since coming into the world.

I want to give you

the most beautiful thoughts

I have ever had since coming into the world.

I want to show you

the best expressions I could produce

since coming into the world.

This is the real reason

why I love you:

my wish to become the best person

in front of you.

끝끝내

너의 얼굴 바라봄이 반가움이다
너의 목소리 들음이 고마움이다
너의 눈빛 스침이 끝내 기쁨이다

끝끝내

너의 숨소리 듣고 네 옆에
내가 있음이 그냥 행복이다
이 세상 네가 살아있음이
나의 살아있음이고 존재이유다.

Ultimately

Looking at your face brings joy.

Hearing your voice inspires gratitude.

Your lightest glance is ultimate joy.

Ultimately,

Hearing you breathing

and being beside you

is simple happiness.

Your being alive in this world

is what makes me alive,

it's my reason for existing.

네가 있어

바람 부는 이 세상
네가 있어 나는 끝까지
흔들리지 않는 나무가 된다

서로 찡그리며 사는 이 세상
네가 있어 나는 돌아앉아
혼자서도 웃음 짓는 사람이 된다

고맙다
기쁘다
힘든 날에도 끝내 살아남을 수 있었다

우리 비록 헤어져
오래 멀리 살지라도
너도 그러기를 바란다.

Since You Are

In this windswept world,

since you are there,

I become a tree that is never shaken.

In this world where people live frowning

at each other, since you are there, I turn

and become someone who smiles all alone.

Thank you.

I am happy.

I was able to survive even on difficult days.

Even if we are separated

and live far apart for a long time,

I hope you will still stay the same.

늦여름

네가 예뻐서
지구가 예쁘다

네가 예뻐서
세상이 다 예쁘다

벗은 발 예쁜 발가락
그리고 눈썹

네가 예뻐서
나까지도 예쁘다.

Late Summer

The Earth is beautiful

because you are so pretty.

The world is beautiful

because you are so pretty.

Bare feet, pretty toes,

and eyebrows.

Even I am pretty

because you are pretty.

별것도 아닌 사랑

사랑 그것, 별것도 아니다

어색하게 손을 잡고 있을 것도 없이
다만 한자리 마주 앉아
가볍게 이야기를 나눈다든가 웃는다든가
그러다가 두 눈을 마주 보며 눈물 글썽이기도 하는 것
그보다 더 큰 것이 아니다

사랑 그것, 멀리 있는 것도 아니다

온다고 하고는 쉽게 나타나지 않는 시간
지루하게 기다리면서 가슴 조린다든가
문득 네가 문을 열고 얼굴 내밀 때
가슴 덜컥 내려앉으면서 반가운 마음
그것에 더가 아니다

혼자 길을 가다가 구름을 보았다든가
바람에 몸을 흔드는 나무를 만났다든가
빈 하늘을 그냥 멍하니 우러를 때

Love, That's Nothing Special

Love, that's nothing special.

Even without awkwardly holding hands,
just sitting opposite each other having a light conversation,
laughing, then looking into each other's eyes and shedding tears.
It's nothing more than that.

And love, that's not something far away.

The times when you say you'll come,
then don't quickly show up
so that my heart aches as I wait idly,
then you suddenly open the door and show your face,
so that my heart calms down and I feel happy.
Nothing more than that.

When you're out walking alone and see clouds,
or when you meet a tree swaying in the wind,

까닭도 없이 코허리가 찌잉해지면서
눈물이라도 번진다면 그것이야말로
가슴속에 사랑이 집을 지었다는 증거

그렇다면, 그렇다면 말이다
사랑 그것은 별것이 아닌 것도 아니다.

or when you just blankly look up at the empty sky,

then your nose starts to tingle for no reason

and tears well up. That's proof

that love has built a home in your heart.

If that's the case, if that's the case,

love cannot be said to be nothing special.

행복 2

어제 거기가 아니고
내일 저기도 아니고
다만 오늘 여기
그리고 당신.

Happiness 2

Not there yesterday,

not over there tomorrow,

but today, here, with you.

유월에

말없이 바라
보아주시는 것만으로도 나는
행복합니다

때때로 옆에 와
서 주시는 것만으로도 나는
따뜻합니다

산에 들에 하이얀 무찔레꽃
울타리에 덩쿨장미
어우러져 피어나는 유월에

그대 눈길에
스치는 것만으로도 나는
황홀합니다

그대 생각 가슴 속에
안개 되어 피어오름만으로도
나는 이렇게 가득합니다.

In June

I am happy

just looking at you

silently.

Sometimes,

just by you coming to stand next to me,

I feel warm

In June, when white wild roses bloom

in the mountains and fields,

and roses bloom in the hedges

I am ecstatic

just by your glance

brushing over me.

Just by thoughts of you

blooming like mist in my heart,

I am full like this.

연

오래
기다리셨습니다

드릴 것은
조그만 마음뿐입니다

부디 오래
머물다 가십시오

바람에겐 듯
사랑에겐 듯.

Lotus

You have been waiting
a long time.

A small heart
is all I have to give you.

Please stay for a long time
before you go.

So to the wind,
so to love.

초라한 고백

내가 가진 것을 주었을 때
사람들은 좋아한다

여러 개 가운데 하나를
주었을 때보다
하나 가운데 하나를 주었을 때
더욱 좋아한다

오늘 내가 너에게 주는 마음은
그 하나 가운데 오직 하나
부디 아무 데나 함부로
버리지는 말아다오.

A Humble Confession

People like it

when I give them what I have.

They like it more

when I give them one of one

than when I give them one of many.

The heart I give you today

is the only one I have.

Please don't just casually throw it away

somewhere.

의자

결코 아름답지 않은 세상
너 한 사람으로 하여
아름다웠다

저만큼 나 다녀오는 동안 너
그 자리 지켜서 좀
기다려줄 수 있겠니?

A Chair

The world that was not at all beautiful

was beautiful

because of you alone.

Will you please stay

just where you are

and wait until I get back?

여행의 끝

어둔 밤길 잘 들어갔는지?

걱정은 내 몫이고
사랑은 네 차지

부디 피곤한 밤
잠이나 잘 자기를…….

Journey's End

Did you find the dark night path safely?

The worries are mine,

the love is yours.

Please sleep well

this weary night...

장식

애당초
못생겨서 좋아했다
뭉뚱한 키 조그만 몸집
찌뿌둥한 얼굴

귀여워서 사랑했다
맑은 이마 부드러운 볼
치렁한 머리칼

언제든 네 조그만 귀에는
새로운 귀걸이를
달아주고 싶었다

언제든 네 머리칼에는
어여쁜 머리핀을
꽂아주고 싶었다.

Decoration

Initially

I liked you because you were not attractive

with that stubby, small body,

sullen face.

I loved you because you were cute

with that clear forehead, soft cheeks,

long hair.

I always longed

to put new earrings

in your small ears,

I always longed

to put a pretty hairpin

in your hair.

그래도

나는 네가 웃을 때가 좋다
나는 네가 말을 할 때가 좋다
나는 네가 말을 하지 않을 때도 좋다
뾰로통한 네 얼굴, 무덤덤한 표정
때로는 매정한 말씨
그래도 좋다.

Still

I like it when you smile.

I like it when you talk.

I like it when you don't talk.

Still, your sulky face, your indifferent expression,

and your sometimes harsh words are also things I like.

좋다

좋아요
좋다고 하니까 나도 좋다.

Good

That's good.

Because you said it's good, it's good for me too.

말랑말랑

공기주머니 너는
산소로 가득한
말랑말랑한

고무풍선 너는
향기로 가득한
야튼 말랑말랑한

너를 안아본다
안아본다는
생각만으로도

가슴이 부푼다
나도 고무풍선이 되어
두둥실 떠오른다

허공이 예쁘다
너 때문에 예쁘다
나도 또한 말랑말랑.

Soft and Fluffy

You are soft and fluffy,
air pockets filled with oxygen;
you are soft and fluffy,
rubber balloons full of fragrance.

I hug you.
Just thinking about hugging you
my heart swells until I become a rubber balloon
and go floating up.

The sky is beautiful.
It's beautiful because of you.
I too am soft and fluffy.

호명

순이야, 부르면
입 속이 싱그러워지고
순이야, 또 부르면
가슴이 따뜻해진다

순이야, 부를 때마다
내 가슴 속 풀잎은 푸르러지고
순이야, 부를 때마다
내 가슴 속 나무는 튼튼해진다

너는 나의 눈빛이
다스리는 영토
나는 너의 기도로
자라나는 풀이거나 나무거나

순이야, 한번씩 부를 때마다
너는 한번씩 순해지고
순이야, 또 한번씩 부를 때마다
너는 또 한번씩 아름다워진다.

Calling Your Name

Suni, when I call you,

my mouth grows fresh,

and when I call you again,

my heart grows warm.

Suni, every time I call you,

the grass in my heart becomes greener,

and when I call you,

the tree in my heart becomes stronger.

You are the territory

governed by my eyes,

I am the grass or the tree

that grows with your prayers.

Suni, every time I call you,

you become gentle once more,

and when I call you again,

you become beautiful once more.

한 사람

쓰러질 듯 비틀거리며 사라지는
나의 뒷모습
안 보일 때까지 바라보아 주는
한 사람

까무러칠 듯 하루의 노동으로부터
돌아와 잠드는 내 얼굴
날이 샐 때까지 지켜보아 주는
한 사람

나중에 나중에
나 세상 떠날 때
망가진 몸과 마음
부드러운 손으로 싸안아 받아주실
오직 한 사람.

One Person

One person

who gazes at my back

as I stagger off and disappear

until they can no longer see it.

One person

who, until the sun rises, watches over my sleeping face

after I stagger back exhausted from a day of work and

fall asleep.

One person

who later, much later,

when I leave this world,

will embrace my broken body and mind

with gentle hands.

모두 떠난 자리에

모두 떠난 자리에
그대 단 하나
내게는 소중한 행운입니다

무너져 내린 가을꽃밭
그대 단 하나
내게는 빛나는 꽃송입니다

바람 부는 산성 위에
오로지 그대
꺾이지 않는 하나의 나무입니다.

The Place Everyone Has Left

In the place everyone has left,

you alone

are my precious fortune

In the withered autumn flowerbed

you alone

are a shining flower for me.

On the windswept mountain fortress,

you alone

are the one tree that will not break.

당신

이 세상 무엇 하러 살았나?

최후의 친구 한 사람
만나기 위해서 살았지

바로 당신.

You

What did you live in this world for?
I lived to meet one last friend.

Yes, you.

사랑은 그런 것

예쁘면 얼마나 예쁘겠나
때로는 나도 내가
예쁘지 않은데

좋으면 얼마나 좋겠나
때로는 나도 내가
좋지 않은데

그만큼 예쁘면 됐지
그만큼 좋으면 됐지
사랑이란 그런 것이다

조금 예뻐도 많이
예쁘다 여겨주면
많이 예뻐지고

조금 좋아도 많이
좋다고 생각하면
많이 좋아지는 것이 아니겠나.

Love Is Like That

How pretty would I be

if I were pretty?

Sometimes I don't think I'm pretty at all.

How good it would be

if I were good.

Sometimes I don't think I'm good at all

It's okay if I'm just so pretty.

It's okay if I'm just so good.

That's what love is

Even if I'm just a little bit pretty,

if I think I'm pretty,

I become very pretty.

Even if I'm just a little bit good,

if I think I'm good,

I become a lot better, right?

사랑에 답함

예쁘지 않은 것을 예쁘게
보아주는 것이 사랑이다

좋지 않은 것을 좋게
생각해주는 것이 사랑이다

싫은 것도 잘 참아주면서
처음만 그런 것이 아니라

나중까지 아주 나중까지
그렇게 하는 것이 사랑이다.

Responding to Love

Love means seeing
unlovely things as lovely.

Love means thinking
not-good things are good.

Tolerating what you don't like,
and not just at the start.

Going on like that until later,
to the end, that's love.

꽃 1

다시 한 번만 사랑하고
다시 한 번만 죄를 짓고
다시 한 번만 용서를 받자

그래서 봄이다.

Flower 1

Let's love once more,

sin once more,

be forgiven once more

It must be spring.

꽃 2

예쁘다는 말을
가볍게 삼켰다

안쓰럽다는 말을
꿀꺽 삼켰다

사랑한다는 말을
어렵게 삼켰다

섭섭하다, 안타깝다,
답답하다는 말을 또 여러 번
목구멍으로 넘겼다

그리고서 그는 스스로 꽃이 되기로 작정했다.

Flower 2

He swallowed lightly
the word, 'Pretty.'

He swallowed in a gulp
the word, 'Pathetic.'

He swallowed with difficulty
the words, 'I love you.'

He swallowed several times
the words, 'Sorry', 'Regret'
and 'Frustrated'.

Then he decided to become a flower himself.

꽃 3

예뻐서가 아니다
잘나서가 아니다
많은 것을 가져서도 아니다
다만 너이기 때문에
네가 너이기 때문에
보고 싶은 것이고 사랑스런 것이고 안쓰러운 것이고
끝내 가슴에 못이 되어 박히는 것이다
이유는 없다
있다면 오직 한 가지
네가 너라는 사실!
네가 너이기 때문에
소중한 것이고 아름다운 것이고 사랑스런 것이고 가득한 것이다
꽃이여, 오래 그렇게 있거라.

Flower 3

It's not because you're pretty.

It's not because you're good.

It's not because you own a lot.

It's just because it's you.

Because you are you,

you are something I want to see,

something I love, something I feel sorry for,

until ultimately you are like a nail in my heart.

There's no reason.

Or if there is one,

it's the fact that you are you!

Because you're you, you're precious and beautiful

loveable and full.

Flower, long may you stay as you are.

한밤중에

한밤중에
까닭없이
잠이 깨었다

우연히 방안의
화분에 눈길이 갔다

바짝 말라 있는 화분

어, 너였구나
네가 목이 말라 나를
깨웠구나.

In the Middle of the Night

I woke up

in the middle of the night

for no reason.

My eyes happened to catch a glimpse

of a flower pot in the room,

A dried-out flower pot.

Oh, it was you!

You woke me up

because you were thirsty.

오늘의 꽃

웃어도 예쁘고
웃지 않아도 예쁘고
눈을 감아도 예쁘다

오늘은 네가 꽃이다.

Today's Flower

You're pretty when you smile,

pretty when you don't smile,

pretty when you close your eyes.

Today, you're a flower.

들길을 걸으며

1
세상에 와 그대를 만난 건
내게 얼마나 행운이었나
그대 생각 내게 머물므로
나의 세상은 빛나는 세상이 됩니다
많고 많은 사람 중에 그대 한 사람
그대 생각 내게 머물므로
나의 세상은 따뜻한 세상이 됩니다.

2
어제도 들길을 걸으며
당신을 생각했습니다.
오늘도 들길을 걸으며
당신을 생각했습니다
어제 내 발에 밟힌 풀잎이
오늘 새롭게 태어나
바람에 떨고 있는 걸
나는 봅니다
나도 당신 앞에 밟히면서

Walking Along a Field Path

1

How lucky I was

to come into the world and meet you.

My world becomes a shining world

because thoughts of you stay with me.

Among many, many people,

you are the one.

My world becomes a warm world

because thoughts of you stay with me.

2

Yesterday, as I walked along a field path

I thought of you.

Today, as I walked along a field path

I thought of you.

I see the blades of grass

that my feet stepped on yesterday

being reborn today and trembling in the wind.

I long to be a blade of grass

새로와지는 풀잎이면 합니다
당신 앞에 여리게 떠는
풀잎이면 합니다.

that becomes new after being stepped on by you.

I want to be a blade of grass

trembling softly before you.

산수유꽃 진 자리

사랑한다, 나는 사랑을 가졌다
누구에겐가 말해주긴 해야 했는데
마음 놓고 말해줄 사람 없어
산수유꽃 옆에 와 무심히 중얼거린 소리
노랗게 핀 산수유꽃이 외워두었다가
따사로운 햇빛한테 들려주고
놀러온 산새에게 들려주고
시냇물 소리한테까지 들려주어
사랑한다, 나는 사랑을 가졌다
차마 이름까진 말해줄 수 없어 이름만 빼고
알려준 나의 말
여름 한 철 시냇물이 줄창 외우며 흘러가더니
이제 가을도 저물어 시냇물 소리도 입을 다물고
다만 산수유꽃 진 자리 산수유 열매들만
내리는 눈발 속에 더욱 예쁘고 붉습니다.

The Place where Cornelian Cherry Blossoms Fell

I love you, I have loved.

I needed to tell someone,

but there was no one I could tell with confidence,

then I came close to the cornelian cherry blossoms

and muttered absentmindedly.

The yellow cornelian cherry blossoms

memorized that and told it to the warm sunlight,

told it to the visiting birds,

even told it to the sound of the stream.

I love you, I have loved.

I didn't tell them your name,

I told them everything, except your name.

The stream kept repeating it all summer,

but now autumn has come to an end,

and the sound of the stream has fallen silent,

only the place where the cornelian cherry blossoms fell,

and the cornelian cherry berries are even more beautiful,

red in the falling snow.

사랑이여 조그만 사랑이여 24

사랑은
안절부절.

사랑은
설레임.

사랑은
서성댐.

사랑은
산들바람.

사랑은
나는 새.

사랑은
끓는 물.

사랑은
천의 마음.

Love, Little Love 24

Love
is restless.

Love
is a fluttering.

Love
is a lingering.

Love
is a breeze.

Love
is a flying bird.

Love
is boiling water.

Love
is a host of hearts.

잠시 머물다 가기에 사랑이다

Lingering for a while then leaving, that is love

안개

흐려진 얼굴

잊혀진 생각

그러나 가슴 아프다.

Fog

Blurred faces,

forgotten thoughts,

a breaking heart.

작별

꽃을 꺾듯이
잡은 채 떨리는 손
떨리는 술잔.

Farewell

As if holding picked flowers,

trembling hands,

trembling wine-glasses.

공항

하루 한나절 헤어져 살아도
잘 가라고 다시 곧 만나자고
뒤돌아보고 손 흔들고 눈 맞추고 그러기 마련인데
그렇게 매몰차게 잡은 손 놓고 돌아서고 말다니
뒤돌아서 다시는 웃는 얼굴조차 보여주지 않다니, 멀어지다니
끝내는 덜커덕 문까지 닫히고 말아
캄캄해진 눈 팍 꺾인 무릎
둘이 왔던 길 어찌 혼자서 돌아갈 수 있었으랴
하늘까지 어둔 하늘
별조차 사라진 하늘 그 아래

나 못 간다, 못 잊는다.

Airport

Even if we are to spend a day or half a day apart,
we look back and wave and make eye contact,
saying Goodbye and See you again soon,
but you let go of the hand that I held so tightly
and turned away, you turned
and never showed me a smile again,
and went far away, and the door finally slammed shut,
and my eyes grew dim, my knees buckled,
how could I go back alone the way we came?
Even the sky is dark, even the stars have disappeared,
under that sky.

I can't go, I can't forget.

별리

우리 다시는 만나지 못하리

그대 꽃이 되고 풀이 되고
나무가 되어
내 앞에 있는다 해도 차마
그대 눈치채지 못하고

나 또한 구름 되고 바람 되고
천둥이 되어
그대 옆을 흐른다 해도 차마
나 알아보지 못하고

눈물은 번져
조그만 새암을 만든다
지구라는 별에서의
마지막 만남과 헤어짐

우리 다시 사람으로는 만나지 못하리.

Separation

We will never meet again,

Even if you become a flower, grass,
or a tree
and stand before me,
I will not notice you.

Even if I become a cloud, wind,
or thunder
and flow by your side,
you will not recognize me

Tears spread
and create a small new spring.
Our last meeting and separation
on the star called Earth.

We will never meet again as people.

바람에게 묻는다

바람에게 묻는다
지금 그곳에는 여전히
꽃이 피었던가 달이 떴던가

바람에게 듣는다
내 그리운 사람 못 잊을 사람
아직도 나를 기다려
그곳에서 서성이고 있던가

내게 불러줬던 노래
아직도 혼자 부르며
울고 있던가.

Asking the Wind

I ask the wind:

Are the flowers still blooming there now?

Has the moon risen?

I listen to the wind:

Is the person I miss, the person I can't forget,

still waiting for me,

lingering there?

Still singing alone the song

sung to me,

crying?

나무

너의 허락도 없이
너에게 너무 많은 마음을
주어버리고
너에게 너무 많은 마음을
뺏겨버리고
그 마음 거두어들이지 못하고
바람 부는 들판 끝에 서서
나는 오늘도 이렇게 슬퍼하고 있다
나무되어 울고 있다.

A Tree

I gave you too much of my heart
without your permission,
and you stole too much of my heart,
and I can't take it back,
so I stand at the end of a windy field
and am sad like this today.
I'm crying like a tree.

그런 사람으로

그 사람 하나가
세상의 전부일 때 있었습니다

그 사람 하나로 세상이 가득하고
세상이 따뜻하고

그 사람 하나로
세상이 빛나던 때 있었습니다

그 사람 하나로 비바람 거센 날도
겁나지 않던 때 있었습니다

나도 때로 그에게 그런 사람으로
기억되고 싶습니다.

Someone Like That

There was a time when that person
was everything in the world to me.

There was a time when the world was filled
with that person, so that the world was warm,

There was a time when the world
was bright when I was with that person.

There was a time when even windy days
were not scary when I was with that person.

Sometimes I also want to be remembered
as someone like that.

사람 그리워

나는 열 번을 죽어 다시 태어나도
사람으로 태어나리
사람 중에서도 사람 그리워
밤잠을 설치고
두 눈이 진무르는
이냥 이대로 못난
사내로 태어나리
그리하여 다시 그대를 만나고
그대와 다시 헤어져
그대 그리워 잠 못 드는 밤을
혼자 가지리.

Longing for People

Even if I die ten times and am reborn,

I will be reborn as a human being.

Among people, I will be reborn as a worthless man

longing for people so much

that I can't sleep at night and my eyes are full of tears.

So I will meet you again,

and I will be separated from you again,

and I will spend sleepless nights alone

longing for you.

섬

너와 나
손잡고 눈 감고 왔던 길

이미 내 옆에 네가 없으니
어찌할까?

돌아가는 길 몰라 여기
나 혼자 울고만 있네.

An Island

You and I, the path we came by,
holding hands,
eyes closed.

What should I do
when you are no longer by my side?

I don't know the way back,
so I am crying here alone.

동백

짧게 피었다 지기에
꽃이다

잠시 머물다 가기에
사랑이다

눈보라 먼지바람 속
피를 삼킨 통곡이여.

The Camellia

Blooming briefly then falling,

that is a flower.

Lingering for a while then leaving,

that is love.

A lament swallowing blood

in snowstorm and dust storm.

인생 3

사막 하나를
사이에 두고

막막한 이쪽과
적막한 저쪽

세상 끝날까지
너와 나.

Life 3

With a desert

between us.

This side vast,

the other side desolate.

You and me

until the end of the world.

사막

처음엔 들판을 뛰어다니던 것들
아침 이슬 속에 빛나는 웃음이었던 것들
더구나 인간의 안쓰러운 사랑이었던 것들

모두가 무너져 평등하게 누워 있다
그럼,
그럼,
그럼,
고개 끄덕이고 있다.

The Desert

The things that first went running over the fields
were the smiles shining in the morning dew,
and even more, the pitiful loves of human beings.

All have collapsed and lie equally.
Yes,
Yes,
Yes,
Nodding.

그래

꽃 피는 봄날에
만나러 오겠다는
말에

그래
그래
그래
그렇게 하자꾸나

'그래'란 말끝에
그렁그렁
맺히는 눈물

보고 싶다
많이
그리고, 고마워.

Yes

When you said

you'd come to see me one spring day

when flowers bloom.

Yes.

Yes.

Yes.

Let's do that.

Tears welling up

at the end of the word 'yes'

I long to see you

so much.

And, thank you.

꽃구경

벚꽃 피면 꽃이 되어 다시 올게요
그 아이 내 앞에서
웃으며 이뤘던 약속

올해도 벚꽃은 피어 만발
흐드러졌는데
벌써 벚꽃들 떠날 채빈데

그 아이 온다는 소식은 없고
혼자 와서 벚꽃나무
올려다보는 날

먼 사람 약속인양 손길인양
벚꽃 잎 나비되어 펄펄
날려라 바람에 하늘에 날려라.

Viewing Flowers

When the cherry blossoms bloom,
I will come back as a flower.
Smiling, a child made that promise to me.

This year, the cherry blossoms
are in full bloom,
they are already preparing to leave,

But there is no news of that child coming,
so one day I come alone
and gaze up at the cherry tree,

Then, like a promise from someone far away,
like a hand waving,
the cherry blossom petals turn into butterflies
and fly up into the sky fluttering, borne on the wind.

제비꽃

그대 떠난 자리에
나 혼자 남아
쓸쓸한 날
제비꽃이 피었습니다
다른 날보다 더 예쁘게
피었습니다.

Violets

One lonely day

in the place from where you set off,

leaving me alone,

violets bloomed.

They bloomed

more beautifully

than on other days.

쓸쓸한 여름

챙이 넓은 여름 모자를 하나
사 주고 싶었는데
그것도 빛깔이 새하얀 걸로 하나
사 주고 싶었는데
올해도 오동꽃은 피었다 지고
개구리 울음 소리 땅 속으로 다 자즈러들고
그대 만나지도 못한 채
또다시 여름은 와서
나만 혼자 집을 지키고 있소
집을 지키며 앓고 있소.

A Solitary Summer

I longed to buy you

a wide-brimmed summer hat,

one that was pure white, but this year

the paulownia flowers have bloomed and fallen,

the croaking of frogs has all fallen into the ground,

summer has come again without my meeting you,

so that I am the only one guarding the house.

I am sick of guarding the house.

붓꽃

슬픔의 길은
명주실 가닥처럼이나
가늘고 길다

때로 산을 넘고
강을 따라가지만

슬픔의 손은
유리잔처럼이나
차고도 맑다

자주 풀숲에서 서성이고
강물 속으로 몸을 풀지만

슬픔에 손목 잡혀 멀리
멀리까지 갔다가
돌아온 그대

오늘은 문득 하늘

Iris

The path of sorrow

is as long and thin

as a silk thread.

Sometimes it crosses mountains

and follows rivers,

But the hand of sorrow

is as cold and clear

as glass.

Often it wanders over grass

and relaxes in a river,

But you,

you have gone far and wide

holding hands with sorrow and returned.

Today, I suddenly see

쪽빛 입술 붓꽃 되어
떨고 있음을 본다.

the sky's blue lips

turned into an iris and trembling.

들국화 1

객기 죄다 제하고
고향 등성이에 와
비로소 고른 숨 골라 쉬며
심심하면
초가집 이엉 위에 드러누워 빨가벗은
박덩이의 배꼽이나 들여다보며
웅얼대는 창자 속 핏덩일랑
아예 말간 이슬로 씻어버리고
그렇지!
시장기 하나로
시장기 하나로
귀 떨어진 물소리나
마음 앓아 들으며
돌아앉아 후미진 산모롱이쯤
내가 우러러도 좋은
이 작은 하늘, 이 작은 하늘아.

Wild Chrysanthemum 1

At the far end of wanderlust

I reach the ridge of my hometown

and finally rest, taking deep breaths,

then when I feel bored

I gaze at the naked belly-button of a gourd

lying on the thatched roof of my house

and sweep away with the limpid dew

the bloody lumps inside my mumbling intestines.

That's right!

With one hunger,

with one single hunger

I listen to the deaf sound of water

and with a heavy heart

sit back and gaze up at the remote mountain ridge,

this small scrap of sky that I can look up to,

this small scrap of sky.

들국화 2

1
울지 않는다면서 먼저
눈썹이 젖어

말로는 잊겠다면서 다시
생각이 나서

어찌하여 우리는
헤어지고 생각나는 사람들입니까?

말로는 잊어버리마고
잊어버리마고……

등피
아래서.

2
살다 보면 눈물날 일도
많고 많지만

Wild Chrysanthemum 2

1

You say you're not crying, but already
your eyebrows are moist.

While your words say you'll forget, still
you remember.

Why are we people who break up,
then still remember?

You say you'll forget,
you'll forget…

But under
the bark…

2

There are very many things in life
that make me cry,

밤마다 호롱불 밝혀
네 강심江心에 노를 젓는
나는 나룻배.

아침이면
이슬길 풀섶길 돌고 돌아
후미진 곳
너 보고픈 마음에
하얀 꽃송이 하날 피웠나부다.

but every night, I am a boat,

I light a lantern,

and row down your river's heart.

When morning comes,

I turn and turn along dewy paths, grassy paths,

then in some sequestered spot

I bloom, one day's white flower,

because I miss you.

들국화 3

바람 부는 등성이에
혼자 올라서
두고 온 옛날은
생각 말자고,
아주 아주 생각 말자고

갈꽃 핀 등성이에
혼자 올라서
두고 온 옛날은
잊었노라고,
아주 아주 잊었노라고

구름이 헤적이는
하늘을 보며
어느 사이
두 눈에 고이는 눈물
꽃잎에 젖는 이슬.

Wild Chrysanthemum 3

I climbed alone

along windswept ridges,

determined not to recall

the old days left behind,

determined never again to recall them.

I climbed alone

along ridges where reeds bloomed,

saying I had quite forgotten

the old days left behind,

had really quite forgotten them.

As I gazed at the sky where clouds went drifting,

before I knew it

tears gathered in my eyes,

dewdrops soaking the petals.

대숲 아래서

1
바람은 구름을 몰고
구름은 생각을 몰고
다시 생각은 대숲을 몰고
대숲 아래 내 마음은 낙엽을 몬다.

2
밤새도록 댓잎에 별빛 어리듯
그슬린 등피에는 네 얼굴이 어리고
밤 깊어 대숲에는 후둑이다 가는 밤 소나기 소리.
그리고도 간간이 사운대다 가는 밤바람 소리.

3
어제는 보고 싶다 편지 쓰고
어젯밤 꿈엔 너를 만나 쓰러져 울었다.
자고 나니 눈두덩엔 메마른 눈물자죽,
문을 여니 산골엔 실비단 안개.

Under the Bamboo Grove

1

The wind yields clouds,

the clouds yield thoughts,

the thoughts yield a bamboo grove.

Beneath the bamboo grove, my heart yields fallen leaves.

2

Just as starlight lingers all night long on the bamboo leaves

your face lingers on the scorched lamp-glass.

As the night passes, there comes a spattering sound of nighttime showers

falling in the bamboo grove, the sound of a night wind gently blowing occasionally.

3

Yesterday, I wrote a letter saying I wanted to see you,

then last night, when I met you in my dreams, I collapsed in tears.

When I woke up, my eyes were filled with dried tears

4

모두가 내 것만은 아닌 가을,
해 지는 서녘구름만이 내 차지다.
동구 밖에 떠드는 애들의
소리만이 내 차지다.
또한 동구 밖에서부터 피어오르는
밤안개만이 내 차지다.

하기는 모두가 내 것만은 아닌 것도 아닌
이 가을,
저녁밥 일찍이 먹고
우물가에 산보 나온
달님만이 내 차지다.
물에 빠져 머리칼 헹구는
달님만이 내 차지다.

and when I opened the door, the mountain valley was full of a silken mist.

4

In autumn, not everything is mine alone.
The western clouds where the sun is setting are mine alone.
The sound of children talking outside the village is mine alone.
The evening mist rising beyond the village is mine alone.

This autumn,
everything is mine and yet not mine.
After an early evening meal
the moon coming out for a stroll by the well
is mine alone.
The moon fallen into the water and rinsing her hair
is mine alone.

재회 1

더 예뻐졌구나
반가움에

강물을 하나 네 앞에
엎을 뻔 했지 뭐냐.

Reunion 1

You've become prettier!
I was so happy

That I almost poured out a river
in front of you.

아직도

아직도 그 전화번호를 쓰고 있었다
아직도 그 번지수에 살고 있었다
봄이 온다고 해서 울컥 치미는 마음
부둥켜안고 전화를 걸었을 때
물먹은 목소리는 아직도 스무 살 서른 같은데
어느새 쉰 살 나이를 넘겼다고 했다
아직도 김지연의 바이올린
'기차는 여덟 시에 떠나네'를
들으며 산다고 그랬다.

Still Now

She was still using that phone number,

she was still living in that house.

When I called her

with a heart full of emotion

because spring was coming,

her voice was still moist

and she said she was still

in her twenties or thirties,

although she was already over fifty.

She said she still listened to Kim Ji-yeon

playing 'The train leaves at eight'

on the violin.

이 가을에

아직도 너를
사랑해서 슬프다.

This Autumn

I'm sad

because I still love you.

그리움 1

햇빛이 너무 좋아
혼자 왔다 혼자
돌아갑니다.

Longing 1

The sunlight is so good,

I came out alone

and will go back home alone.

그리움 2

때로 내 눈에서도
소금물이 나온다
아마도 내 눈 속에는
바다가 한 채씩 살고 있나 보오.

Longing 2

Sometimes salt water

flows from my eyes.

Might there be a sea

living in each of my eyes?

그리움 3

가지 말라는데 가고 싶은 길이 있다
만나지 말자면서 만나고 싶은 사람이 있다
하지 말라면 더욱 해보고 싶은 일이 있다

그것이 인생이고 그리움
바로 너다.

Longing 3

There is a path that I want to take even though I'm told not to
There is a person that I want to meet even though I'm told not to
There is something that I want to do more if I'm told not to.

That's life and longing.
It's you.

이별

있네
있네
아직도 있네
웃는 얼굴

없네
없네
금방 없네
우는 얼굴.

Parting

There is,

there is,

there is still a smiling face

There is not,

there is not,

there soon will not be,

a crying face.

오늘도 그대는 멀리 있다

Today, too, You Are Far Away

바람 부는 날

너는 내가 보고 싶지도 않니?
구름 위에 적는다

나는 너무 네가 보고 싶단다!
바람 위에 띄운다.

A Windy Day

Don't you want to see me?
I write on the clouds.

I so want to see you!
I go flying on the wind.

부탁

너무 멀리까지는 가지 말아라
사랑아

모습 보이는 곳까지만
목소리 들리는 곳까지만 가거라

돌아오는 길 잊을까 걱정이다
사랑아.

A Request

Don't go too far away,

Love.

Just go as far as we can see each other

and hear our voices

I'm worried you'll forget the way back,

Love.

사는 법

그리운 날은 그림을 그리고
쓸쓸한 날은 음악을 들었다

그리고도 남는 날은
너를 생각해야만 했다.

How to Live

On days when I missed you, I drew.

On days when I felt lonely, I listened to music.

And on the remaining days,

I just had to think about you.

떠나와서

떠나와서 그리워지는
한 강물이 있습니다
헤어지고 나서 보고파지는
한 사람이 있습니다
미루나무 새 잎새 나와
바람에 손을 흔들던 봄의 강가
눈물 반짝임으로 저물어가는
여름날 저녁의 물비늘
혹은 겨울 안개 속에 해 떠오르고
서걱대는 갈대숲 기슭에
벗은 발로 헤엄치는 겨울 철새들
헤어지고 나서 보고파지는
한 사람이 있습니다
떠나와서 그리워지는
한 강물이 있습니다.

After Leaving

There is a river that I miss after leaving it.

There is someone I long to see after parting.

A spring riverside where new leaves of the poplar trees

sprout and wave their hands in the wind.

A summer evening's sunset ripples sparkling like tears.

A winter migratory bird walking barefoot

on the shore of a rustling reedbed.

The sun rising in winter fog.

There is someone I long to see after parting.

There is a river that I miss after leaving it.

오지 못하는 마음

신발
신발 바닥이 많이
닳았겠다

내가 너를 기다리는 동안
너 또한 내게로 오지 못해
문밖에 서서

바장이다가
안달하다가
끝내 오지 못하는 마음

다시 신발이나
한 켤레 사서
너에게 보내줄까 그런다.

A Heart That Can't Come

Your shoes,

the soles of your shoes, must be worn out.

While I'm waiting for you,

standing outside the door,

but you can't come to me.

A heart that is fretting,

impatient for you

who are unable to come.

Should I buy

another pair of shoes

and send them to you?

사랑하는 마음 내게 있어도

사랑하는 마음
내게 있어도
사랑한다는 말
차마 건네지 못하고 삽니다
사랑한다는 그 말 끝까지
감당할 수 없기 때문

모진 마음
내게 있어도
모진 말
차마 하지 못하고 삽니다
나도 모진 말 남들한테 들으면
오래오래 잊혀지지 않기 때문

외롭고 슬픈 마음
내게 있어도
외롭고 슬프다는 말
차마 하지 못하고 삽니다
외롭고 슬픈 말 남들한테 들으면

Even Though I Have a Loving Heart

Even though I have a loving heart,

I live without being able to say

'I love you'

because I can't bear to say

'I love you'.

Even though I have a harsh heart,

I live

without being able to utter

harsh words.

Because if I hear harsh words from others,

I won't forget them for a long time.

Even though I have a lonely, sad heart,

I live

without being able to say

'I'm lonely and sad,'

because if I hear lonely sad words from others,

I'll become lonely and sad too.

나도 덩달아 외롭고 슬퍼지기 때문

사랑하는 마음을 아끼며
삽니다
모진 마음을 달래며
삽니다
될수록 외롭고 슬픈 마음을
숨기며 삽니다.

I live

cherishing my loving heart.

I live

soothing my harsh heart.

I live

hiding my lonely and sad heart as much as possible.

미루나무

바람 부는 날에도
흔들리지 않음은
마음속에 네가 들어와
살기 때문

아니지

바람 불지 않는 날에도
혼자 몸 흔들며 울고 있는
키 큰 미루나무 한 그루
키우고 있기 때문.

The Willow Tree

I am not shaken
even on windy days
because you have come
and live in my heart.

Not so

It's because
I'm raising a tall willow tree
that shakes and cries alone
even on windless days.

개양귀비

생각은 언제나 빠르고
각성은 언제나 느려

그렇게 하루나 이틀
가슴에 핏물이 고여

흔들리는 마음 자주
너에게 들키고

너에게로 향하는 눈빛 자주
사람들한테도 들킨다.

Poppies

Thoughts are always fast,

awakening is always slow.

That's how blood collects in my chest

over a day or two.

My wavering heart

is often caught by you.

My eyes looking at you

are often caught by other people.

편지

기다리면 오지 않고
기다림이 지쳤거나
기다리지 않을 때
불쑥 찾아온다
그래도 반가운 손님.

A Letter

If you wait, it won't come,

and when you're tired of waiting

or when you're no longer waiting,

it suddenly comes,

ever, a welcome guest.

부탁이야

오래가 아니야 조금
많이가 아니야 조금
네 앞에서 잠시
앉아있고 싶어

나는 왜 내가 이렇게 되었는지
나도 잘 모르겠어

금방 보고 헤어졌는데도
보고 싶은 네 얼굴
금방 듣고 돌아섰는데도
듣고 싶은 네 목소리

어둔 하늘 혼자서 반짝이는 나는 별
외론 산길에 혼자서 가는 나는 바람

웃는 네 얼굴 조금만 보고
예쁜 목소리 조금만 듣고
이내 나는 떠나갈 거야

Please

Not for long, just a little,
not a lot, just a little
I want to sit before you
for a moment.

I really don't know
why I've become like this.

Your face that I long to see
although we just saw each other before parting,
your voice that I long to hear
although I have only just turned away.

As I twinkle alone in the dark sky, I am a star.
As I walk alone on a mountain path, I am the wind.

I will leave soon,
after seeing your smiling face for just a moment,
after hearing your pretty voice for just a moment,

그렇게 해줘 부탁이야

나는 왜 내가 이렇게 되었는지
나도 잘 모르겠어.

so please let me go.

I really don't know

why I've become like this.

그 말

보고 싶었다
많이 생각이 났다

그러면서도 끝까지
남겨두는 말은
사랑한다
너를 사랑한다

입속에 남아서 그 말
꽃이 되고
향기가 되고
노래가 되기를 바란다.

Those Words

I missed you so much,

I often thought about you

And yet, the words

that remained until the end were,

I love you,

I love you.

I hope those words

will remain in my mouth

and become a flower,

a fragrance, a song.

오늘도 그대는 멀리 있다

전화 걸면 날마다
어디 있냐고 무엇하냐고
누구와 있냐고 또 별일 없냐고
밥은 거르지 않았는지 잠은 설치지 않았는지
묻고 또 묻는다

하기는 아침에 일어나
햇빛이 부신 걸로 보아
밤사이 별일 없긴 없었는가 보다

오늘도 그대는 멀리 있다

이제 지구 전체가 그대 몸이고 맘이다.

Today, too, You Are Far Away

When we phone, every day,

you ask me where I am, what I am doing,

who I am with, and if I am okay,

if I skipped meals,

if I am having trouble sleeping.

Well, judging from the sunlight shining brightly

when I wake up in the morning,

I guess nothing happened overnight.

Today, too, you are far away.

Now, the entire Earth is your body, your heart.

마지막 기도

더 이상 그를
사랑하지 않게 해주십시오
사랑하는 마음이 언젠가
미움의 마음으로 변할까 걱정입니다

어떤 경우에도 그를
미워하지 않게 해주십시오
그를 사랑했던 마음
오래 오래 후회될까봐 걱정입니다.

Last Prayer

Please let me

not love her anymore.

I'm worried that my love

will turn into hate someday

Please don't let me hate her

under any circumstances

I'm worried that my heart's love

will last a long time and I'll regret it.

멀리서 빈다

어딘가 내가 모르는 곳에
보이지 않는 꽃처럼 웃고 있는
너 한 사람으로 하여 세상은
다시 한 번 눈부신 아침이 되고

어딘가 네가 모르는 곳에
보이지 않는 풀잎처럼 숨 쉬고 있는
나 한 사람으로 하여 세상은
다시 한 번 고요한 저녁이 온다

가을이다, 부디 아프지 마라.

Praying from Afar

Because somewhere, I don't know where,
you are there, just you, smiling like an invisible flower,
once again the world knows a dazzling morning.

Because somewhere, somewhere you don't know,
I am there, just me, breathing like an invisible blade of grass,
once again the world knows a quiet evening,

It's autumn. I pray you won't fall sick.

겨울에도 꽃 핀다

온다 온다 하면서도
못 온다
간다 간다 하면서도
못 간다

그래도 좋아
너는 여전히
내 마음속에 와서 살고
나도 여전히
네 마음속에 가서
살고 있을 테니까

이제 또다시 겨울
그래도 나는
꽃을 피운다
네 생각으로 순간순간
꽃을 피운다

너도 부디 꽃을 피워라

Flowers Bloom Even in Winter

You say you're coming, you're coming,

but can't come,

I say I'm going, I'm going,

but can't go.

But that's okay,

because you'll still come

and live in my heart

and I'll still go

and live in your heart

Now it's winter again,

but I'll still bloom.

I'll bloom flowers

moment by moment

thinking of you.

Please bloom, you too,

a flower that doesn't exist in the world,

세상에는 없는 꽃
아무도 모르는 꽃
아직은 이름도 없는 꽃.

a flower that no one knows about,

a flower that doesn't even have a name yet.

연꽃

마음을 좀 보여달라고 그러자
말없이 보오얀 맨발을 뽑아 보여주는
한 아낙이 있었습니다

봄비에 미나리빛 웃음 하나로
봄비에 미나리빛 웃음 하나로

그때부터
조바심하지 않고 그 아낙을
그리워할 수 있게 되었습니다.

A Lotus

There was a woman who,
when I asked her to show me her heart,
silently bared her white feet and showed them to me.

With a smile as green as water parsley in spring rain.
With a smile as green as water parsley in spring rain.

From that moment on,
I grew able to yearn for that woman
without feeling impatient.

내가 너를

내가 너를 얼마나
좋아하는지
너는 몰라도 된다

너를 좋아하는 마음은
오로지 나의 것이요,
나의 그리움은
나 혼자만의 것으로도
차고 넘치니까……

나는 이제
너 없이도 너를
좋아할 수 있다.

I and You

It's okay

if you don't know

how much I like you.

The way my heart likes you

is my affair alone,

and if my yearning

is full to overflowing,

that too is only my affair…

I can like you

now

without you.

안부

오래
보고 싶었다

오래
만나지 못했다

잘 있노라니
그것만 고마웠다.

Greetings

I have been longing to see you
for a long time.

I haven't seen you
for a long time.

I just feel thankful
that you're doing well.

꽃이 되어 새가 되어

Becoming a Flower, Becoming a Bird

꽃이 되어 새가 되어

지고 가기 힘겨운 슬픔 있거든
꽃들에게 맡기고

부리기도 버거운 아픔 있거든
새들에게 맡긴다

날마다 하루해는 사람들을 비껴서
강물 되어 저만큼 멀어지지만

들판 가득 꽃들은 피어서 붉고
하늘가로 스치는 새들도 본다.

Becoming a Flower, Becoming a Bird

If you have a sorrow that is hard to bear,
entrust it to the flowers.

If you have a pain that is hard to handle,
entrust it to the birds.

Every day, the sun avoids people,
turns into a river, and goes far away

But the fields are crimson, full of blooming flowers,
and I see birds flying across the sky.

풀꽃 1

자세히 보아야
예쁘다

오래 보아야
사랑스럽다

너도 그렇다.

Wildflower 1

Look closely.

It's so pretty.

Take a long look.

It's so lovely.

Like you.

풀꽃 2

이름을 알고 나면 이웃이 되고
색깔을 알고 나면 친구가 되고
모양까지 알고 나면 연인이 된다
아, 이것은 비밀.

Wildflower 2

When you know the name, you become a neighbor.

When you know the color, you become a friend.

When you know the shape, you become a lover.

Ah, that's a secret.

풀꽃 3

기죽지 말고 살아봐
꽃 피워봐
참 좋아.

Wildflower 3

Don't be discouraged, live.

As flowers bloom.

That's really good.

혼자서

무리지어 피어 있는 꽃보다
두 셋이서 피어 있는 꽃이
도란도란 더 의초로울 때 있다

두 셋이서 피어 있는 꽃보다
오직 혼자서 피어있는 꽃이
더 당당하고 아름다울 때 있다

너 오늘 혼자 외롭게
꽃으로 서 있음을 너무
힘들어 하지 말아라.

Alone

There are times

when just two or three flowers blooming together

are more harmonious than flowers blooming in clusters.

There are times

when one flower blooming alone

is more elegant and beautiful than two or three flowers

blooming together.

Don't be too unhappy if today

you stand alone,

lonesome as a solitary flower.

앉은뱅이꽃

발밑에 가여운 것
밟지 마라,
그 꽃 밟으면 귀양간단다.
그 꽃 밟으면 죄받는단다.

A Squat Flower

That poor little thing underfoot!

Don't step on it!

If you step on that flower, you'll be exiled.

If you step on that flower, you'll be punished.

봄비

사랑이 찾아올 때는
엎드려 울고

사랑이 떠나갈 때는
선 채로 울자

그리하여 너도 씨앗이 되고
나도 씨앗이 되자

끝내는 우리가 울울창창
서로의 그늘이 되자.

Spring Rain

When love comes,

let's lie down and cry

When love leaves,

let's stand up and cry

So let's you become a seed

and I become a seed.

Let's end up becoming

each other's deep shadows.

어린 벗에게

그렇게 너무 많이
안 예뻐도 된다

그렇게 꼭 잘하려고만
하지 않아도 된다

지금 모습 그대로 너는
충분히 예쁘고

가끔은 실수하고 서툴러도 너는
사랑스런 사람이란다

지금 그대로 너 자신을
아끼고 사랑해라

지금 모습 그대로 있어도
너는 가득하고 좋은 사람이란다.

To a Young Friend

You're all right,

even without being so very pretty.

You don't have to try so hard to do well.

You are pretty enough just as you are now.

Even if sometimes you make mistakes

and are clumsy, you are still lovable.

Love and cherish yourself

just as you are now.

You are a full and good person

just the way you are now.

너무 잘하려고 애쓰지 마라

너, 너무 잘하려고 애쓰지 마라
오늘의 일은 오늘의 일로 충분했다
조금쯤 모자라거나 비뚤어진 구석이 있다면
내일 다시 하거나 내일
다시 고쳐서 하면 된다
조그마한 성공도 성공이다
그만큼에서 그치거나 만족하라는 말이 아니고
작은 성공을 슬퍼하거나
그것을 빌미 삼아 스스로를 나무라거나
힘들게 하지 말자는 말이다
나는 오늘도 많은 일들과 만났고
견딜 수 없는 일들까지 견뎠다
나름대로 최선을 다한 셈이다
그렇다면 나 자신을 오히려 칭찬해주고
보듬어 껴안아줄 일이다
오늘을 믿고 기대한 것처럼
내일을 또 믿고 기대해라
오늘의 일은 오늘의 일로 충분했다
너, 너무도 잘하려고 애쓰지 마라.

Don't Try too Hard

You must not try too hard.

Today's tasks were enough for today.

If there's something that's a little lacking or crooked,

you can do it again tomorrow or fix it tomorrow.

Even small successes are successes

That doesn't mean you should stop there or be satisfied.

Don't be sad about small successes or use them

as an excuse to scold yourself or make life hard for yourself.

I encountered many things today, even endured unbearable things,

but I did my best in my own way,

so I should praise myself, embrace myself, hug myself,

believe in and look forward to tomorrow

just as you believed in and looked forward to today.

Today's tasks were enough

You must not try too hard.

꽃필 날

내게도
꽃필 날 있을까?
그렇게 묻지 마라

언제든
꽃은 핀다

문제는
가슴의 뜨거움이고
그리움, 기다림이다.

The Day Flowers Bloom

Will I have a day

when flowers bloom?

Don't ask that

Flowers bloom anytime.

The problem is

the warmth of the heart,

the longing, the waiting.

잘람잘람

어머니, 어머니
샘물가에서 물동이로
물을 기를 때

물동이에 가득 채운 물
머리에 이고 가기 전
넘치지 않게 하기 위하여
물동이 주둥이를 손바닥으로
슬쩍 훑어내듯이

오늘 내가 너에게
주는 마음은 잘람잘람
그렇지만 넘치지 않게

오늘 내가 너에게
주는 시도 잘람잘람
그렇지만 넘치지 않게.

Brimming

Mother, Mother
When you draw water
from a spring with a jar,

Just as you lightly sweep
the mouth of the jar with your palm
before carrying it on your head,
to prevent it from overflowing,

The heart I give you today
is brimming,
but not overflowing.

The poem I give you today
is brimming,
but not overflowing.

아끼지 마세요

좋은 것 아끼지 마세요
옷장 속에 들어 있는 새로운 옷 예쁜 옷
잔칫날 간다고 결혼식장 간다고
아끼지 마세요
그러다 그러다가 철지나면 헌옷 되지요

마음 또한 아끼지 마세요
마음속에 들어 있는 사랑스런 마음 그리운 마음
정말로 좋은 사람 생기면 준다고
아끼지 마세요
그러다 그러다가 마음의 물기 마르면 노인이 되지요

좋은 옷 있으면 생각날 때 입고
좋은 음식 있으면 먹고 싶은 때 먹고
좋은 음악 있으면 듣고 싶은 때 들으세요
더구나 좋은 사람 있으면
마음속에 숨겨두지 말고
마음껏 좋아하고 마음껏 그리워하세요

Don't Be Stingy

Don't be stingy about good things.
Don't be stingy about wearing the new clothes
in your closet, the pretty clothes, saying
you'll wear them when going to a party, going to a wedding.
As time passes they'll wear out, become old clothes.

Don't be stingy about your heart.
Don't be stingy with the loving heart,
the yearning heart that you have in your heart, saying
you'll give it when you come across a really good person.
As time passes your heart will dry up, grow old.

If you have good clothes, wear them whenever you think of them,
and if you have good food, eat it whenever you want to,
and if you have good music, listen to it whenever you want to.
Moreover, if you have a good person, don't hide that in your heart,

그리하여 때로는 얼굴 붉힐 일
눈물 글썽일 일 있다한들
그게 무슨 대수겠어요!
지금도 그대 앞에 꽃이 있고
좋은 사람이 있지 않나요
그 꽃을 마음껏 좋아하고
그 사람을 마음껏 그리워하세요.

but like them as much as you want, yearn for them as much as you want.

So what's the big deal
if you blush or shed tears sometimes?
Aren't there flowers and good people in front of you now?
Like those flowers as much as you want,
yearn for those people as much as you want.

좋은 날 하자

오늘도 해가 떴으니
좋은 날 하자

오늘도 꽃이 피고
꽃 위로 바람이 지나고

그렇지, 새들도 울어주니
좋은 날 하자

더구나 멀리 네가 있으니
더욱 좋은 날 하자.

Let's Have a Good Day

The sun has risen today,
so let's have a good day.

The flowers are blooming today,
the wind is blowing over the flowers,

And the birds are singing too,
so let's have a good day.

And since, far away, you are there,
let's have an even better day.

좋은 날

하고 싶은 일을 하니 좋고
하고 싶지 않은 일을 하지 않으니
더욱 좋다.

A Good Day

If you do what you want to do, that's good.
If you don't do what you don't want to do,
that's even better.

게으름 연습

텃밭에 아무 것도 심지 않기로 했다
텃밭에 나가 땀흘려 수고하는 대신
낮잠이나 자 두기로 하고
흰 구름이나 보고 새소리나 듣기로 했다

내가 텃밭을 돌보지 않는 사이
이런저런 풀들이 찾아와 살았다
각시풀, 쇠비름, 참비름, 강아지풀,
더러는 채송화 꽃 두어 송이
잡풀들 사이에 끼어 얼굴을 내밀었다
흥, 꽃들이 오히려 잡풀들 사이에 끼어
잡풀 행세를 하드느는군

어느 날 보니 텃밭에
통통통 뛰어 노는 놈들이 있었다
메뚜기였다 연초록빛
방아깨비, 콩메뚜기, 풀무치 어린 새끼들도 보였다
하, 이 녀석들은 어디서부터 찾아온 진객들일까

Practicing Laziness

I decided not to plant anything in the garden.
I decided to take a nap and just look at the white clouds
and listen to the birds singing
instead of going out into the garden and sweating.

While I was not tending to the garden,
all sorts of weeds came to live there.
Wildflowers, sedges, common sedges, dogtails,
and sometimes a couple of rose moss
poked their faces out between the weeds.
Huh, flowers are trying to sneak in between the weeds,
pretending to be weeds!

One day, I saw some guys bouncing around in the garden.
They were grasshoppers.
There were light green grasshoppers, locusts, and baby locusts.
Ha, where did these guys come from?

내가 텃밭을 돌보지 않는 사이
하늘의 식솔들이 내려와
내 대신 이들을 돌보아 주신 모양이다
해와 달과 별들이 번갈아 이들을 받들어
가꾸어 주신 모양이다

아예 나는 텃밭을 하늘의
식솔들에게 빌려주기로 했다
그 대신 가끔 가야금이든
바이올린이든 함께 듣기로 했다.

While I was not tending to the garden,

it seemed a whole family had come down from the sky

and taken care of it instead of me.

It seemed that the sun, moon, and stars

had taken turns supporting and cultivating it.

I left the garden to the family from the sky.

I decided to lend it to them.

Instead, I decided to listen to a gayageum

or violin together with them sometimes.

꽃밭에서

뽑으려 하니
모두가 잡초였지만

품으려 하니
모두가 꽃이었습니다.

In the Flowerbed

When I tried to pull them up,
they were all weeds,

but when I tried to embrace them,
they were all flowers.

오늘의 약속

덩치 큰 이야기, 무거운 이야기는 하지 않기로 해요
조그만 이야기, 가벼운 이야기만 하기로 해요
아침에 일어나 낯선 새 한 마리가 날아가는 것을 보았다든지
길을 가다 담장 너머 아이들 떠들며 노는 소리가 들려 잠시 발을 멈췄다든지
매미 소리가 하늘 속으로 강물을 만들며 흘러가는 것을 문득 느꼈다든지
그런 이야기들만 하기로 해요

남의 이야기, 세상 이야기는 하지 않기로 해요
우리들의 이야기, 서로의 이야기만 하기로 해요
지나간 밤 쉽게 잠이 오지 않아 애를 먹었다든지
하루 종일 보고픈 마음이 떠나지 않아 가슴이 뻐근했다든지
모처럼 개인 밤하늘 사이로 별 하나 찾아내어 숨겨놓은 소원을 빌었다든지
그런 이야기들만 하기로 해요

실은 우리들 이야기만 하기에도 시간이 많지 않은 걸 우리는 잘 알아요

Today's Promise

Let's not tell big stories, heavy stories.
Let's only tell small stories, light stories.
Like when you wake up in the morning
and see a strange bird flying by,
like when you hear the sound of children playing
and talking beyond the fence
as you stop for a moment while walking down the street,
like when you suddenly sense the sound of cicadas
flowing up into the sky like a river.
Let's only tell those stories

Let's not tell other people's stories, the world's stories.
Let's only tell our own stories, each other's stories,
like when you couldn't fall asleep easily last night and had a hard time,
like when you couldn't stop missing me all day long and your heart ached,
like when you finally found a star in the clear night sky and made a secret wish.

그래요, 우리 멀리 떨어져 살면서도
오래 헤어져 살면서도 스스로
행복해지기로 해요
그게 오늘의 약속이에요.

Let's only tell those stories.

Actually, we know very well
that we don't have much time to talk about just ourselves.
Yes, even though we live far apart,
even though we have lived apart for a long time,
let's be happy on our own.
That's today's promise.

선물 1

하늘 아래 내가 받은
가장 커다란 선물은
오늘입니다

오늘 받은 선물 가운데서도
가장 아름다운 선물은
당신입니다

당신 나지막한 목소리와
웃는 얼굴, 콧노래 한 구절이면
한 아름 바다를 안은 듯한 기쁨이겠습니다.

Gift 1

The greatest gift

I have ever received here below

is today.

Among the gifts

I have received today,

the most beautiful gift is you

Your soft voice, smiling face,

and a single humming phrase

are a joy like embracing the ocean in armfuls.

오늘

지금 여기
행복이 있고

어제 거기
추억이 있고

멀리 저기에
그리움 있다

알아서 살자.

Today

Here and now

there is happiness .

Yesterday

there is memory.

Far away

there is longing.

Let's live understanding that.

행복 1

저녁 때
돌아갈 집이 있다는 것

힘들 때
마음속으로 생각할 사람 있다는 것

외로울 때
혼자서 부를 노래 있다는 것.

Happiness 1

Having a home to return to
in the evening.

Having someone to think of
when times are tough.

Having a song to sing alone
when you're lonely.

그럼에도 불구하고

지금 사람들 너나없이
살기 힘들다, 지쳤다, 고달프다
심지어 화가 난다고까지 말을 한다

그렇지만 이 대목에서도
우리가 마땅히 기댈 말과
부탁할 마음은 '그럼에도 불구하고'

그럼에도 불구하고 우리는
밥을 먹어야 하고
잠을 자야 하고 일을 해야 하고

그럼에도 불구하고 우리는
아낌없이 사랑해야 하고
조금은 더 참아낼 줄 알아야 한다

무엇보다도 소망의 끈을
놓치지 말아야 한다
기다림의 까치발을 내리지 말아야 한다

Nonetheless

Without exception, people these days say
that life is hard, that they're tired, exhausted,
and even that they're angry.

However, in this respect,
the words we should rightly stress,
the attitude we should seek are 'Nonetheless'

Nonetheless we have to eat,
we have to sleep,
we have to work.

Nonetheless we have to know how to love
unreservedly and
how to endure just a little bit longer.

Above all, we must not lose
the bond of hope.
We must not let give up waiting on tiptoe.

그것이 날마다 아침이 오는 까닭이고
봄과 가을 사계절이 있는 까닭이고
어린것들이 우리와 함께하는 이유이다.

That is why every new morning comes,

why there are spring and autumn among the four seasons,

and why we have children with us.

그가 섭섭하게 대해 줄 때

그가 섭섭하게 대해 줄 때
그가 내게 잘해 준 일만을 생각합니다
그가 미워하는 마음을 가질 때
그가 나를 위해 기도해 준 일을 생각합니다
그가 크게 실망하고 슬퍼할 때
그가 작은 일에도 기뻐하던 때를 되새깁니다
그가 늙고 병들어 보잘것없어질 때
그가 젊어 예쁘던 때를 기억하겠습니다.

When They Treat Me Badly

When they treat me badly,

I think only of the good things they have done for me.

When they have hateful hearts,

I think of the prayers they have prayed for me.

When they are greatly disappointed and sad,

I recall the times when they were happy over small things.

When they become old and sick and good for nothing,

I will remember the days when they were young and pretty.

뒷모습 1

얼굴이 예쁜 사람은 불행하다
자기 눈으로 예쁜 자기의 모습을
볼 수 없기 때문
뒷모습이 예쁜 사람은 더욱 불행하다
더욱이나 자기 눈으로는
예쁜 뒷모습을 볼 수 없기 때문
그러나 얼굴이 예쁜 사람은 행복하다
자기의 예쁜 얼굴을
세상에 예쁘지 않은 사람들에게 보여 줌으로
다른 사람들을 기쁘게 하기 때문
뒷모습이 예쁜 사람은
더욱 행복하다
자기는 볼 수 없는 뒷모습을
항상 다른 사람들에게 숨김없이
드러내놓기 때문.

Back view 1

People with pretty faces are unhappy

because they can't see their pretty faces

with their own eyes.

People with pretty backs are even more unhappy

since they can't see their pretty backs

with their own eyes.

However, people with pretty faces are happy

because they make others happy

by showing their pretty faces

to the world's unpretty people.

People with pretty backs are even happier

because they always reveal their backs,

which they can't see,

to others without hiding anything.

노래 방울

비 오는 날이지
날이 어둡고 우울하지
짜증도 나지
그렇다고 마음까지
비에 젖으면 안 되지

마음에 젖어드는 물방울들
튕겨내야지
튕겨내더라도 세차게 힘차게
리드미컬하게 튕겨내야지
통, 통, 통, 통
그래, 비 오는 소리로 말이야
어두운 마음 우울한 마음은 모두
빗방울이 가져가라고
빗방울에게 맡겨야지
끝내 우리는 환하고 밝은
맑은 날을 가슴에 품어야지

그래, 노래 방울이 되어야지

Song Drops

It's a rainy day,

a dark and gloomy day.

It's annoying

but you shouldn't let your heart

get soaked with rain on that account.

You have to brush off the water droplets

that are soaking your heart.

When you brush them off,

you have to brush them off energetically,

powerfully, rhythmically.

Tong-tong, tong-tong.

Yes, with the sound of rain,

we have to entrust

all our dark and gloomy hearts

to the raindrops

so that they can take them away.

Ultimately, we have to embrace

멀리까지 가는 메아리의 숲
새소리의 터널이 되어야지
얼마나 좋겠니?

a bright and clear day in our hearts.

In fact, we have to become song drops.

We have to become a forest of echoes
that travel far,
a tunnel of bird song.
How good that would be.

산수유

아프지만 다시 봄

그래도 시작하는 거야
다시 먼 길 떠나보는 거야

어떠한 경우에도 나는
네 편이란다.

Cornelian Cherry

It may hurt, but it's spring again.

So let's start,
let's set out on a long journey again.

In any case, I'm
at your side.

너는 별이다

남을 따라서 살 일이 아니다
네 가슴에 별 하나
숨기고서 살아라
끝내 그 별 놓치지 마라
네가 별이 되어라.

You Are a Star

No need to imitate other people in life.

Live with the star

hidden in your heart.

Never lose that star.

Become a star yourself.

지친 마음 곁에 피어난 풀꽃 한 송이

박재섭(인제대 명예교수, 국문학)

나태주는 1971년 서울신문 신춘문예로 등단한 이후 오늘날까지 지속적으로 시작詩作 활동을 해오면서 탁월한 예술적 성취를 이룬 현대 한국의 대표적 시인이다. 당시 신춘문예 심사위원이었던 박목월 시인은 다음과 같이 그를 소개했다.

"나 군은 한국의 전통적인 서정시를 계승하여 오늘의 것으로 빚어 놓은 희귀한 시인이다. 그의 알찬 열매는 어느 것이나 오늘의 것으로서의 참신성과 신선미를 잃지 않고 있으며, 그의 작품은 누구에게나 친근감과 신선감을 베풀어주리라고 확신한다." (나태주 시집 『대숲 아래서』의 서문 중)

일찍이 박목월은 나태주가 한국 시단의 큰 재목으로 성장할 것임을 깊은 통찰력으로 예감했던 것이다. '시의 아버지'였던 스승 박목월의 기대에 어긋나지 않게 그는 평생 시

창작의 외길을 걸어왔으며, 현재까지 출간한 창작시집은 50권을 넘어섰다. 가히 소월-지용-목월의 시 정신을 계승하여 한국 근현대 시의 맥을 이어가고 있다고 해도 과언이 아닐 것이다.

1. 짧기에 더욱 깊은 울림

"자세히 보아야 예쁘다 / 오래 보아야 사랑스럽다 / 너도 그렇다."(〈풀꽃1〉 전문) 광화문의 한 생명보험 회사가 25년 동안 건물 외벽에 걸어둔 글판에서, 나태주 시인의 「풀꽃1」이 가장 큰 사랑을 받았다고 한다. 퇴근 후 지친 몸을 이끌고 집으로 돌아가는 수많은 사람들에게 미소를 짓게 한 이 시는 이제 모든 한국인의 마음속에 자리 잡은 국민시가 되었다. 그리고 그를 풀꽃 시인으로 부르게 했다.

이 시는 단 세 줄, 20음절 남짓한 짧은 형식임에도 강렬한 여운을 남긴다.

"너도 그렇다"라는 마지막 구절은 독자 각자가 자신의 경험과 감정을 대입하도록 하여 보편적인 감동을 끌어낸다. 극도의 간결성과 함축미는 나태주 시의 핵심 매력이다. "시의 언어는 가장 적은 단어로 최대한의 의미를 담아야 한다."라는 에즈라 파운드의 말처럼 그의 시는 삶의 진실을 농축된 시어로 형상화하고 있다.

"많이 보고 싶겠지만 / 조금만 참자."(《묘비명》 전문)의 구절은 가장 간결하다는 17음절의 일본 하이쿠보다 더 짧다. 담담한 어조의 내밀한 독백은 미래에 대한 섣부른 계획보다 오늘의 생활에 충실하고자 하는 웅숭깊은 지혜로 독자를 끌어들인다. "어머니는 언제 죽나? / 내가 죽을 때 죽지."(《동행》 전문)라는 시 역시 최소한의 단어로 긴 여운을 남기며 짧은 시의 매력을 극대화한다. 간결성과 함축성은 독자의 집중력과 긴장감을 높인다. 짧은 구절로 시선을 사로잡고 반전과 반복을 통해 예상치 못한 의미 전환을 만들어 강렬한 인상을 준다.

이런 반전反轉적 구성은 영화감독 세르게이 에이젠슈타인의 충돌적 몽타주를 연상케 한다. 에이젠슈타인이 정적이고 동적인 이미지의 대비를 통해 감정적 충격을 유발했듯이, 나태주의 시 역시 평범한 표현 속에서 갑자기 깊은 깨달음이나 반전을 주어 독자에게 깊은 여운을 남긴다. "만나기는 한나절이었지만 / 잊기에는 평생도 모자랐다."(《시3》 전문)에서는 짧은 순간과 긴 시간이라는 대조를 통해 시적 긴장을 형성한다. 이는 충돌적 몽타주의 방식처럼 예상치 못한 전환을 통해 의미를 극대화하는 효과를 갖는다. 즉, 나태주의 짧은 시에서 발견되는 반전은 단순한 스타일이 아니라, 독자에게 깊은 정서적 경험을 전달하는 핵심적인 장치로 작용하는 것이다.

2. 마음의 보석 발견하기

"그냥 줍는 것이다 / 길거리나 사람들 사이에 / 버려진 채 빛나는 / 마음의 보석들."(《시2》 전문)에서 보듯 나태주 시인은 일상적인 소재와 상황을 통해 삶의 본질적인 가치를 탐구한다. 길가의 풀꽃, 바람에 흔들리는 나뭇잎, 석양, 노을 등 평범한 풍경 속에서 그는 아름다움과 의미를 발견하고, 이를 시적 언어로 승화시킨다. 이러한 작업은 독자에게 익숙한 일상을 새로운 시각으로 바라보게 하며, 잊고 있던 감각과 감성을 되살리는 계기를 제공한다. 윌리엄 블레이크는 "한 알의 모래에서 세계를 보고, / 한 송이 들꽃에서 천국을 본다."고 하며 작은 것들 속에 담긴 심오하고 거대한 의미를 강조했다. 나태주의 시들이야말로 사소한 일상 속에서 보편적인 진실을 발견한다.

시인은 일상의 사소한 순간들을 포착해 독자에게 친근하게 다가간다. 일상의 한 장면, 한 생각이 간결하게 그려지고, 독자는 자신의 일상과 자연스럽게 연결 짓는다. 「시1」에서 "마당을 쓸었습니다 / 지구 한 모퉁이가 깨끗해졌습니다"라는 구절은 평범한 행동이 세계와 연결되고 있음을 강조하며, 일상적인 행위가 지닌 깊은 의미를 전달한다. 또한 「내가 좋아하는 사람」에서는 "남의 앞에 섰을 때 / 교만하지 않고 / 남의 뒤에 섰을 때 / 비굴하지 않은 사람."과 같이 보통 사람들의 가치관을 담아내며 독자들에게 친숙하게 다가간다.

"시들은 나에게 약이 되어주었습니다. 마음의 약입니다. 영혼의 상처를 다스려주는 약이고 거친 마음을 달래주는 약입니다. 그래서 나는 사람을 살리는 시를 생각합니다. 사람의 마음을 쓰다듬어 주고 늘어진 어깨를 일으켜주는 시를 생각합니다. 그야말로 사람과 동행하는 시들입니다."(나태주 엮음시집 『시가 나에게 살라고 한다』의 서문 〈시가 사람을 살립니다〉 중)

이 인용은 나태주 시인이 지향하는 시 창작의 본질이 '상처의 치유'임을 명확히 드러낸다. 현대인들은 디지털 기술의 발달과 과학적 예측의 증가로 인해 과거의 집착과 미래의 불안 속에서 현재의 행복을 놓치며 살아간다. 철학자 알랭 드 보통은 저서 『불안』에서 '우리가 느끼는 불안은 대개 과거의 후회와 미래의 걱정으로부터 기인한다.'고 진단하며,

지나친 시간에 대한 집착이 현재를 살아갈 힘을 앗아간다고 지적했다.

바로 이러한 맥락에서 오늘의 독자들에게 나태주의 시가 큰 호소력을 갖는 것은, 그의 시들이 〈오늘, 여기〉를 환기하는 치유의 힘 덕분이다. 「행복 1」에서는 "저녁 때 / 돌아갈 집이 있다는 것 / 힘들 때 / 마음속으로 생각할 사람이 있다는 것"이라는 구절로 삶의 평범한 일상이 주는 소중함을 강조하여, 현재 누릴 수 있는 행복과 감사의 가치를 깨닫게 한다.

「선물 1」에서 나태주는 "하늘 아래 내가 받은 / 가장 커다란 선물은 / 오늘입니다"라고 표현하여 오직 현재에 집중하는 삶의 자세를 제안하고, 「아끼지 마세요」에서는 매순간을 충일한 삶의 밀도로 지낼 것을 다음과 같이 노래한다. "마음 또한 아끼지 마세요 / 마음속에 들어 있는 사랑스런 마음 그리운 마음 / 정말로 좋은 사람 생기면 준다고 / 아끼지 마세요 / 그러다 그러다가 마음의 물기 마르면 노인이 되지요"

이처럼 나태주의 시들은 과거와 미래라는 시간의 함정에 빠져 불안을 겪는 오늘날의 현대인들에게, 현재의 삶에 머물며 일상의 작은 행복을 발견하고 감사할 수 있도록 따뜻한 치유의 언어로 다가가고 있다.

3. 자기 긍정의 힘

나태주 시에 내재되어 있는 또 하나의 치유력은 그의 시들이 갖고 있는 내적 성찰과 자기 긍정의 힘이다. 철학자 에리히 프롬은 『사랑의 기술』에서 '타인을 사랑하기 위해서는 무엇보다 자기 자신을 먼저 사랑할 수 있어야 한다.'고 강조한 바 있는데, 나태주 시의 화자는 바로 이러한 자기애와 성찰의 중요성을 지속적으로 일깨운다. 그의 시 「풀꽃 2」에서 시인은 "이름을 알고 나면 이웃이 되고 / 색깔을 알고 나면 친구가 되고 / 모양까지 알고 나면 연인이 된다"고 말하며 타인과 관계를 맺는 시작점이 자신에 대한 성찰과 타인에 대한 이해에서 비롯된다는 것을 일깨운다.

또한 「내가 너를」이라는 시에서 시인은 "내가 너를 얼마나 좋아하는지 / 너는 몰라도 된다 / 너를 좋아하는 마음은 오로지 나의 것이요, / 나의 그리움은 나 혼자만의 것으로도 차고 넘치니까…"라는 구절로 자기 안에서 우러난 사랑의 감정이 타인에 대한 진정한 사랑으로 확장될 수 있음을 보여준다. 이처럼 나태주의 시들은 시적 화자의 깊은 자기 성찰과 자기애를 바탕으로 하며, 이는 정신분석학자 칼 융이 '자신의 내면을 성찰하고 긍정할 때 비로소 타인과 세상을 진정으로 수용할 수 있다.'고 주장한 것과 같은 맥락에 놓여 있다.

요컨대 나태주 시의 치유력은 그의 시가 단순한 위로를

넘어, 삶의 본질적인 질문을 던지고 독자 스스로 답을 찾아가도록 돕는 데서 비롯된다. 그의 시는 독자에게 삶의 아름다움과 슬픔을 동시에 경험하게 하며, 이를 통해 내면의 상처를 치유하고 삶의 긍정적인 측면을 발견하도록 이끈다.

연애편지로 시작된 그의 시는 평생토록 세상과 교감하는 사랑의 편지가 되었고, 스승 박목월을 만나 더욱 빛을 발했다. 그의 말대로 시는 곧 세상에게 보내는 사랑의 편지이기에, 나태주 시인은 오늘도 그 편지를 통해 독자들의 마음에 작은 위안과 희망의 씨앗을 심고 있다. 자신의 시를 읽는 모든 이들이 삶의 성장과 치유를 얻기를 바라는 그는, 말 그대로 모든 사람들이 시를 좋아하는 세상을 꿈꾸는 시인이다. 나태주의 삶과 철학에서 우러나온 시 세계는 그래서 더욱 따뜻하고 깊이 있게 우리 곁에 다가온다. 짧지만 깊고, 간결하지만 강렬한 감동을 주는 그의 시는 현대 독자들에게 큰 울림을 전한다. 특히 그의 짧은 시들은 SNS와 같은 디지털 플랫폼에서 빠르게 공유되며, 짧은 문구 속에 담긴 깊은 의미가 현대 사회의 바쁜 일상 속에서도 독자들에게 즉각적인 공감과 위로를 선사한다. 독자와 함께 걷고 함께 호흡하는 '사람과 동행하는 시'로서, 오늘도 많은 사람들의 마음을 위로하고 성장시키며 살아 숨 쉬고 있음을 지적해 두고 싶다.

역자 안선재 수사는 오랜 시간 한국 문학의 아름다움을 세계에 알리는 데 헌신해온 탁월한 번역가이다. 그 역시 나태주 시인처럼 묵묵히 번역 작업의 외길을 40년 이상 걸어왔다. 이 번역 시집을 통해 전 세계 독자들이 나태주의 따뜻한 시적 감성을 경험하며 마음의 치유와 위로를 얻을 수 있기를 기대한다.

A Wildflower Blooming Next to a Tired Heart

Park Jae-seop (Emeritus Professor,
Korean Literature, Inje University)

Na Tae-ju is a leading poet of contemporary Korea who has achieved outstanding artistic achievements while continuously writing poetry since his debut in the *Seoul Shinmun* New Year's Literary Contest in 1971. The poet Park Mok-wol, who was a judge for the New Year's Literary Contest at the time, introduced him as follows:

"Mr. Na is a rare poet who has inherited traditional Korean lyric poetry and shaped it into something for today. All his rich fruits have lost none of their originality and freshness as something of today, and I am confident that his works will provide familiarity and freshness to everyone." (From the preface to Na Tae-ju's poetry collection, 'Under the Bamboo Grove')

Park Mok-wol had a deep insight that Na Tae-ju would grow into a great talent in Korean poetry. Living up to the expectations of his teacher, the 'father of modern Korean poetry,' Na has devoted his life to writing poetry, and has published over fifty volumes of his own poetry. It would not be an exaggeration to say that he has inherited the spirit of the founding fathers of modern Korean poetry and is continuing the pulse of modern and contemporary Korean poetry.

1. Deeper resonance because short

"Look closely. / It's so pretty. / Take a long look. / It's so lovely. / Like you." (full text of 'Wildflower 1'). It is said that Na Tae-ju's 'Wildflower 1' received much love because of a signboard bearing it that a life insurance company in Gwanghwamun had hanging on the exterior wall of its building for 25 years. This poem, which brought a smile to countless people who were dragging their tired bodies home after work, has now become a national poem that has taken root in the hearts of all Koreans. And it has led him to be called the 'Wildflower Poet.'

This poem, which is only three lines and about twenty syllables long, leaves a strong aftertaste. The last phrase, "Like you." draws out universal emotions by allowing each reader to substitute their own experiences and emotions. Extreme brevity and conciseness are the core charms of Na Tae-ju's poetry. As Ezra Pound said, "The language of poetry is so dense, so multivalent." His poetry embodies the truth of life in condensed poetic language.

The phrase "You must long to see me again, / but let's wait a little longer." (full text of 'Epitaph') is shorter than the 17-syllable Japanese haiku, which is often said to be the most concise form of poem. The calm tone and intimate monologue draw readers in with the profound wisdom of wanting to be faithful to today's life rather than making hasty plans for the future. The poem, "When will Mother die? / She will die when I die." (full text of 'Companionship') also maximizes the charm of short poems by leaving a long aftertaste with minimal words. Conciseness and implication increase the reader's concentration and tension. It captures the attention with short phrases and creates an unexpected change of meaning through reversal and repetition, leaving a strong impression.

This reversal composition is reminiscent of the conflicting montages of film director Sergei Eisenstein. Just as Eisenstein caused emotional shock through the contrast of static and dynamic images, Na Tae-ju's poetry also leaves a deep aftertaste with the reader by suddenly giving deep realization or reversal in ordinary expressions. "We only met for half a day, / but a lifetime was not long enough to forget." (full text of 'Poem 3') creates poetic tension through the contrast of a short moment and a long time. This has the effect of maximizing meaning through unexpected transitions, like the method of conflicting montages. In other words, the reversal found in Na Tae-ju's short poems is not a simple style, but a key device that conveys deep emotional experiences to readers.

2. Discovering the jewels of the heart

As seen in "I'm just picking up / The sparling jewels

of the heart abandoned in the streets or among the crowds." (full text of 'Poem 2'), poet Na Tae-ju explores the essential value of life through everyday materials and situations. In ordinary scenery such as roadside flowers, leaves swaying in the wind, and sunset glows, he discovers beauty and meaning, and sublimates them into poetic language. This work allows readers to look at familiar daily life from a new perspective, and provides an opportunity to revive forgotten senses and emotions. William Blake emphasized the profound and enormous meaning contained in small things, saying, "To see a world in a grain of sand, / and a Heaven in a wild flower." Na Tae-ju's poems truly discover universal truths in trivial daily life.

The poet captures small moments of daily life and approaches readers in a friendly way. A scene from everyday life, a thought is concisely depicted, and readers naturally connect it to their own daily lives. In his 'Poem 1,' the phrase "I swept the yard. / A corner of the Earth became clean" emphasizes that ordinary actions are connected to the world, and conveys the deep meaning of everyday actions. Also, in 'The

Person I Like', the values of ordinary people are captured, such as "Someone not arrogant / when standing before others, / not servile / when standing behind others." and readers are familiar with them.

"Poems have been my medicine. They are medicine for the heart. They are medicine that heals the wounds of the soul and soothes the rough heart. That's why I think of poetry that saves people. I think of poetry that comforts people's hearts and lifts up sagging shoulders. These are poems that truly accompany people." (From the prolog "Poetry saves people" to Na Tae-ju's compiled poetry collection, 'Poetry tells me to live')

This quote clearly reveals that the essence of poet Na Tae-ju's poetry creation is 'healing wounds'. Modern people live missing out on present happiness amidst their obsession with the past and anxiety about the future, due to the development of digital technology and the increase in scientific predictions. In his book 'Satus anxiety', philosopher Alain de Botton diagnosed that 'anxiety stems from a combination of regrets about the past and worries about the future' and pointed out that excessive obsession with time robs us of the strength to live in the present.

It is in this context that Na Tae-ju's poetry has such great appeal to today's readers because of the healing power of his poems that evoke today, here. In 'Happiness 1', Na Tae-ju emphasizes the preciousness of ordinary daily life with the phrase "Having a home to return to / in the evening. / Having someone to think of / when times are tough." and makes us realize the value of happiness and gratitude that we can enjoy in the present.

In 'Gift 1', Na Tae-ju says, "The greatest gift / I have ever received here below / is today." By expressing it as "today," he suggests a life attitude that focuses only on the present, and in 'Don't Be Stingy', he sings about living every moment with the density of a full life. "Don't be stingy about your heart. / Don't be stingy with the loving heart, / the yearning heart that you have in, saying / you'll give it when you come across a really good person. / As time passes your heart will dry up, grow old."

In this way, Na Tae-ju's poems approach modern people who are trapped in the time trap of the past and the future and suffer from anxiety, with warm healing language so that they can stay in the present life and discover and be grateful for the small happiness in everyday life.

3. The Power of Self-Affirmation

Another healing power inherent in Na Tae-ju's poetry is the power of internal reflection and self-affirmation that his poems have. In "The Art of Loving," philosopher Erich Fromm emphasized that 'in order to love others, you must first be able to love yourself,' and the speaker of Na Tae-ju's poems continuously emphasizes the importance of this self-love and reflection. In his poem 'Wildflower 2,' the poet says, "When you know the name, you become a neighbor. / When you know the color, you become a friend. / When you know the shape, you become a lover," reminding us that the starting point of forming relationships with others comes from self-reflection and understanding of others.

Also, in the poem 'I and You,' the poet shows that the feeling of love that arises within oneself can expand into true love for others with the phrase, "It's okay / if you don't know how much I love you. / The way my heart like you is my affair alone, / and if my yearning is full to overflowing, / that too is only my affair..." In this way, Na Tae-ju's poems are based on the deep self-reflection and self-love of the poetic speaker, and this is in the same context as what psychoanalyst Carl Jung said, 'self-reflection and acceptance of one's inner self are crucial for genuine acceptance of other and the world.'

In short, the healing power of Na Tae-ju's poetry comes from the fact that his poetry goes beyond simple comfort and asks essential questions about life and helps readers find answers on their own. His poetry allows readers to experience the beauty and sadness of life at the same time, and through this, heals their inner wounds and leads them to discover the positive aspects of life.

His poetry, which began as a love letter, became a love letter that has communicated with the world throughout his life, and it became even more brilliant after meeting his teacher Park Mok-wol. As he said, poetry is a love letter to the world, and so poet Na Tae-ju continues to plant small seeds of comfort and hope in the hearts of his readers through his letters today. He is a poet who dreams of a world where everyone loves poetry, hoping that everyone who reads his poetry will experience growth and healing in life. The world of poetry that comes from Na Tae-ju's life and philosophy comes to us all the more warmly and deeply. His short but deep, concise but intensely moving poems resonate deeply with modern readers. In particular, his short poems are quickly shared on digital platforms such as SNS, and the deep meaning contained in short phrases provides immediate sympathy and comfort to readers even in the busy daily lives of modern society. As a 'poem that accompanies people' that walks and breathes with readers, I would like to point out that it is alive and breathing today, comforting and growing the hearts of many people.

Translator Brother Anthony is an excellent translator who has devoted a long time to introducing the beauty of Korean literature to the world. Like poet Na Tae-ju, he has also silently walked the lonely path of translation work for over 40 years. I hope that readers around the world will experience Na Tae-ju's warm poetic sensibility and find healing and comfort in their hearts through this translated poetry collection.

사랑한다, 나는 사랑을 가졌다

초판 1쇄 발행 2025년 5월 8일

지은이 나태주
번역 안선재

발행인 이진희, 강한록
발행처 파랑
출판등록 2024년 7월 3일(제 2024-000028호)
주소 충청남도 천안시 서북구 시청로39 113-403
전화 070.4571.5017 **팩스** 0504.296.7360
이메일 jinhee-lee@parangbooks.com
www.instagram.com/parang_books
ISBN 979-11-991175-0-1 03810

ⓒ 나태주 · 안선재, 2025

이 책의 영문번역저작권은 역자와의 독점계약으로 '파랑'이 소유합니다.
저작권법에 의하여 보호를 받는 저작물이므로 무단전재 및 복제를 금합니다.

I love you, I have loved

First edition, First publishing May 8, 2025

Written by Na Tae-ju
Translated by Brother Anthony of Taizé

Publisher Lee Jinhee, Kang Hanrog
Publishing Company Parang
Address 113-403, Sicheong-ro39, Seobuk District, Cheonan City,
South Chungcheong Province, Republic of Korea
Tel +82.70.4571.5017 **Fax** +82.504.296.7360
E-mail jinhee-lee@parangbooks.com
www.instagram.com/parang_books
ISBN 979-11-991175-0-1 03810

ⓒ Na Tae-ju · Brother Anthony of Taizé

The English translation copyright of this book is owned by 'Parang'
through an exclusive contract with the translator.
This work is protected by copyright law, so unauthorized reproduction
and copying are prohibited.